The Art of Prophecy

The Art of Prophecy

A How–To Guide from Beyond the Grave by Amos, a Major Minor Prophet

DAVID BREEDEN

Foreword by Wally Swist

RESOURCE *Publications* · Eugene, Oregon

THE ART OF PROPHECY
A How–To Guide from Beyond the Grave by Amos,
a Major Minor Prophet

Copyright © 2021 David Breeden. All rights reserved. Except for brief quotations in critical publications or reviews, no part of this book may be reproduced in any manner without prior written permission from the publisher. Write: Permissions, Wipf and Stock Publishers, 199 W. 8th Ave., Suite 3, Eugene, OR 97401.

Resource Publications
An Imprint of Wipf and Stock Publishers
199 W. 8th Ave., Suite 3
Eugene, OR 97401

www.wipfandstock.com

PAPERBACK ISBN: 978-1-6667-0201-9
HARDCOVER ISBN: 978-1-6667-0202-6
EBOOK ISBN: 978-1-6667-0203-3

06/08/21

Being a collection of poems, sayings, scriptures, prophecies, musings, and rants by Amos, who may perhaps be in a (somewhat) better place.

File under: #justice, #divinity, #hereafter, #humanism, #creativity, and other #imponderables.

For the prophets & the poets scattered among the stones and stories.

What matters is not to know the world but to change it.
—Frantz Fanon

To see clearly is poetry, prophecy, and religion—all in one.
—John Ruskin

Though we do not wholly believe it yet, the interior life is a real life, and the intangible dreams of people have a tangible effect on the world.
—James Baldwin

Contents

Foreword by Wally Swist | ix

Preface | xiii

Part I: IN THE VALLEY OF DECISION | 1

Part II: PENULTIMATE ANSWERS TO ULTIMATE QUESTIONS | 103

Part III: WHAT IS STRUGGLING TO BE BORN? | 175

About the Author | 237

Foreword

by Wally Swist

It is apt that one of the several quotes from a variety of notable authors prefacing David Breeden's *The Art of Prophecy: A How-To Guide from Beyond the Grave by Amos, a Major Minor Prophet* would include the French philosopher Alain Badiou, a colleague of Gilles Deleuze and Michael Foucault, who writes about such concepts as *truth* not being either *postmodern* or a simple repetition of the concept of *modernity,* and whose philosophy just may be expressed succinctly by the quote used here, "Justice does not exist, which is why we must create it." A minor prophet from the Bible, Amos was an eight century BCE shepherd and dresser of sycamore trees, who was discerning enough to point up the differences of the ruling elite and take issue with it.

It is Amos whom Breeden gives voice in poems that are reminiscent of William Carlos Williams, written in American idiom, as well as epistolary prose poems that conjure the work of Russell Edson. However, David Breeden's poetry is refreshingly his own, as in these lines from the poem "A Resume from the Other End of the Spectrum" in which Amos concretizes his criticism of the upper class, "Thataway, where the fattest parasites/ themselves. Where the high/ 'n mighty sat, attached, sucking// our blood. Thataway where a new/ Pharaoh always sits, looking to lion/ us all up like so many lamed// sheep." Lines such as these are also evocative of Edward Dorn's persona poems in his book *Gunslinger,* considered to be one of the best long poems of the 1960s.

And as Breeden has Amos himself quoting Foucault, we as readers sit up straighter so we can best listen to the depths of truth found in these poems, "Truth is a thing of this world, produced only by virtue of multiple forms of constraint." But as Breeden may know Badiou and Foucault, he knows his own soul and the soul of man when he writes so eloquently of the spiritual rigors of silence, "As I said, the one thing you learn in the desert night is silence. You develop one of those intimate relationships with silence. Roaring, deafening silence. Makes some tell stories. Makes some sing songs. Makes some hear things."

Breeden, who has also adapted Laozi's *Daodejing* (Lamar University Press, 2015), includes Verse 23 from this Eastern classic in this book, and offers much wisdom here in these lines, "When we make The Way our study/ Those attempting to practice it/ Agree with us, and those attempting/ To pursue it agree with us, &/ Even those failing to attempt it// Agree with us.// But when we stop/ Our own attempts/ All others lose faith in us." What Breeden is illustrating through Laozi is the spiritual law that we are not only all connected, and ostensibly all *One*, but not unlike the concept of *Antahkarana*, developed by Elizabeth Claire Prophet, which is essentially "the web of life" or specifically "the net of light spanning Spirit and Matter connecting and sensitizing the whole of creation within itself and to the heart of God." What Breeden posits is that it is on us and within us—all our acts and thoughts and how we focus our will is our largest asset and our most formidable strength, that everything counts, and as the prolific Native American poet Carroll Arnett, or *Gogisgi*, once Chief of the Overhill Band of the Cherokee Nations, once wrote, "Everything counts/ and nothing happens fast."

Breeden also makes use of a kind of dialect that made the *Pogo* comic strip popular and vivid, as in the eponymous character's well-known phrase, "we have met the enemy and he is us." This kind of American patois works to portray Joan of Arc and make her contemporary, "Ask Sister Joan D'Arc, speaking of *par examples* & the peasantry & all. She'll tell you: Getting to the place of speaking truth is a costly little process. Your whole darn dirt–poor domestic servant gene pool is going to add up to the truth you tell. & when you're comin' from there, ain't nobody gonna listen. You're gonna get yer bum fried."

Another example of this use of dialect, which appears throughout the book, is when Amos is speaking lyrically about truth, both then and now, since these are notes to us from the other side, and Breeden's poetry is poignant, even unfortunately timeless:

> "Sycamore pruner."
> Makes me sound like I was out
> in somebody's garden trimming
> trees for an extra buck.

> No. Out in the hedgerows
> cutting the damnedest
> poorest excuse for a fig–like
> something that there is.
> Just to sell something to
> poor folks so that they feel
> like they've eaten something
> like the rich folks, who buy
> figs as an afterthought."

Also, *Confessions of a Minor Prophet* is not without virtuoso imagistic turns, such as the following example, from "Thanks for Asking (a rantette)," with Amos once again soliloquizing: "That I was all kinds of ersatz and cardboard back in my carbon–based days. Admit it. That's what you think . . . . A shadow play in a cardboard factory."

Actually, Breeden develops what can be termed a doxological lyricism in this book-length poem that is also dialectical and intrinsic to an ontological phenomenology in which he constructs a language that is both poetical metaphysical at once, and perhaps in doing so paying homage to both Martin Heidegger and Gaston Bachelard, as in these lines from "The Primate Paradox," which are some of the best lines in the book:

> "Any word contains
> other words in its
> meaning & is
> only part of
> a system of words.
> For every action
> there is the choice;
> there is the action;
> then there is
> the interpretation.
> Every emotion has
> a story, a history.
> Human beings cannot act
> outside of human nature—
> all human actions
> are human nature."

There is also a palpable echo of D. A. Levy, whom Gary Snyder fashioned an entire essay about in his book, *The Old Ways* (New Directions, 1977). The essay regarding this little known Cleveland poet who flourished in the mid-1960s is entitled "The Dharma Eye of D. A. Levy,"

Foreword

and Breeden exercises his own "dharma eye" in a poem such as "I See You," which additionally reveals one of the richer veins in a work that is significant to look at both as a whole and in part due to its containing a number of sparkling gems—as did the *oeuvre* of D. A. Levy as is indicated by Gary Snyder in his essay.

> "Look, the days are coming, YHWH says,
> when the plowman shall overtake the reaper,
> & the treader of grapes the sower;
> & the mountains will drop sweet wine,
> & all the hills will melt.
> & I will bring my people of Israel out of captivity,
> & they will rebuild the wasted cities & inhabit them;
> & they will plant vineyards,
> & drink the wine from them;
> they shall also make gardens,
> & eat the fruit from them.
> I shall plant them upon their land,
> & they shall be pulled up no more
> out of their land
> which I have given them,
> YHWH says so."

David Breeden makes his book-length persona poem about Amos a work of visionary and prophetic beneficence—perhaps worthy of the announcement of a newly amended New Testament.

Wally Swist
(author of *Evanescence: Selected Poems,* Shanti Arts, 2020)
August 2020, South Hadley, Massachusetts

Preface

The biblical canon classifies "Amos, the book of . . ." as the words of a minor Hebrew prophet. The book he wrote—if he wrote it—is short & was later revised by someone else. (Or perhaps someone-s else.) Amos lived—if he lived—in the mid–700s BCE.
A long time ago. And no time at all.

Born in the southern kingdom of Judah, his call to prophecy was to the north, in Israel. The mid–700s BCE was a time of prosperity for some in Israel and Judah. This was the problem Amos addressed: as old tribal structures crumbled, only a few at the top of the social ladder enjoyed prosperity.

Amos came from the back country; he was a sheep herder and dresser of sycamore trees.

There is speculation as to where and how he died. The following is more speculation: what if there's an afterlife of sorts? What if Amos is there? What if he is somehow jotting some notes and passing them along?

Unless otherwise noted, all translations & adaptations are the work of the author. Note that, while most of the text of the *Book of Amos* is contained in these pages, the text is not in its biblical order.

PART I

In the Valley of Decision

Multitudes, multitudes,
in the valley of decision!
For the Day of YHWH is near
in the valley of decision.

(JOEL 3:14)

For at any price we must keep those who have too clear a conscience from living and dying in peace.

—EMIL M. CIORAN

Justice does not exist, which is why we need to create it.

—ALAIN BADIOU

Here are the words of Amos, born among the shepherds of Tekoa. These words concern Israel in the reigns of King Jeroboam II of Israel & King Uzziah of Judah. Amos spoke two years before the earthquake, saying this . . .

> You wanna be
>   a major minor like me?
> Here's how!

The Situation

Once there was a kingdom
very much like any kingdom,
meaning its people
were very much like
you & me. Everybody.

Meaning neither better
nor worse than the people
of any other kingdom

(this makes a difference
to the story) . . .

The leaders of the kingdom
were like the leaders
of any other kingdom,
meaning they wanted
to be known as great
leaders but mostly they
were not great but
wanted more. More

riches. More persons to
rule. More victories.
More land, expanding borders.
More. & more. & more.

(This makes a difference

The Art of Prophecy

to the story) . . .
This kingdom was like
any other kingdom,
meaning the people were
like every other people—

they wished to be people
of virtue; they hoped to be
remembered and timeless;
they tried to be clever, but

mostly they wanted more.
& more. & more & more
different kinds of more.

(This makes a difference
to the story) . . .

These people in this kingdom
had an idea of the sacred—

they had their g–d who
wished them to be—virtuous,
they thought. Which is a fine
thought as far as thinking goes.

Their g–d also wanted more,
but on good days the people
thought this *more* concerned

virtue. Being & doing a little
better. But some had told them
what this YHWH wanted was
to be worshiped in *just this way*.

Face it: some guy's fantasy.

In this way their divinity
was much like every other

The Situation

divinity, meaning their divinity
was much like the divinity
imagined by you or me.

(It always does make a difference
that everything, everywhere
is like everywhere else.)

It makes a difference
in how we see how
everything is very much
like you & me. Everybody.

Like everyone, they worshiped
some other g–ds too.

Into this kingdom came
a prophet preaching that
the people of the kingdom
were much like all the people
in all the other kingdoms,

but that they could be better,
not because they *were* better,
but because they could act

more justly. & the prophet
told them what this looked like:

Not enriching their leaders,
or more-ing in their land, or
more-ing & much-ing themselves
& their worship & rites
but by being *kind*.

Compassionate.

Imagine that. Being kind. Being
just. Sharing their more & their

The Art of Prophecy

more with all the people.

In this the prophet
was like most other prophets
& the people like
most other people . . .

talking a lot;
listening not at all.

Here's For Real For Ya

You do get it, don't you, that the existence or not of g-ds has no consequence or meaning in the category of discussing the motivation of carbon-based creatures to do the right thing.

The conjuring lies in the inspiration brought to bear by pre-existing assumptions. Prophets pull the triggers on pre-loaded guns. The existence and the motivation lie in using symbols and meanings in such as way that people get fired up and act in good-for-everybody sorts of ways.

For real: I don't care what kicks you in the arse and gets you doing the right thing. All I care about is kicking you in the arse. The carrot of heaven. The stick of hell. The carrot and stick of conviction that improving the lot of others is a meaning and purpose to carbon existence. I don't care. I don't give a tinker's damn. All I want is to kick you in the arse.

The End is Near!

Everybody I meet asks, "Where the hell is Tekoa?"

I have to say, "Where I'm from. But I have no idea anymore." You know, Rome never was what it used to be and all that.

I mean, maybe I could find it on a map. By tripping through familiar place names, places still named the same as when I wandered the earth as a carbon-based creature, places I've gone through on the way from here to there. Maybe. But, I only passed most ways once in this world, while I was still carbon.

I don't think I care enough to bother finding Tekoa, though. Really, I doubt it. I doubt I could be brought close enough to caring to bother.

You see, I'm not a carbon-based life form anymore. I'm dead.

And so far, the afterlife is entertaining enough, I suppose. It appears to be a test I haven't passed, but I'm not really interested enough to explore the problem.

Or study for the answers.

For me—someone sort of dead I mean—the afterlife—or wherever I am—is a city with lots of pubs. No dancing allowed. But I can't dance anyhow.

Wherever I am is full of nearly-famous people and a few superstars. Sometimes, someone just disappears— poof! Nobody knows where they go. We all assume it's to a better place because . . . why not? Heck, after

The End is Near!

you've served your time as a carbon-based creature, mystery and not knowing are a way of life, am I right?

But who knows? This existence I'm in—if that's what it is—looks a lot like the carbon-based one, really. Except the pubs never close and don't have cash tills.

You carbon-based beings don't know where you are either, am I right? Then one day, poof! You're somewhere else.

Yeah. Just let me tell you—when you get there . . . here . . . you won't know where you are either. Or why. Or where you're going next. But, heck, we're accustomed to that. It's existential, ya know.

We all see that "poof!"

And we wonder. Just like the carbon-based playthings of time.

But most of all, we do stuff. And remember.

Actually, here, on long afternoons, nobody much wants to hear where you're from. Or the distance you've come. Who the hell cares? Maybe, especially, you know . . . yourself.

That's not the point. Geography is not the point.

For me, my carbon got gathered up into a particular heap in Tekoa. It's a bloody little place. Killing & revenge killing. & then some more killing. A place of murders & justification for murders. A place of zealotry. A place with no imagination at all.

A dull, haunted, bloody place, Tekoa. Ever was; ever has been. Ever will . . . I suppose, but . . . . But I was there in the 750s. Before my bro Jesus was born.

Well, fate appears to be unwritten. Which I think is important, as you, dear carbon-based reader, shall see if you read on.

The Art of Prophecy

Fate appears to be unwritten. Yet writ in stone. And not. Change, in other words, is hard. Which you know already.

Yet, somehow, life's clichéd end is almost inevitable, given the nature of carbon-based creatures.

Tekoa.

A lot like the human mind, isn't it?

What a bloody little place!

Let's Just Set the Scene Here

I don't know if I can really write a how-to on being a major minor prophet. You'll see how I did it. Take it or leave it.

One thing you need to know if you plan on being a live prophet instead of a dead one: Never turn your back on a priest. I got murdered by one. By a priest, I mean, from Bethel. "Beth-El," the "House of G-d." Oh, the irony.

But when you've been around as long as I have, what *ain't* irony?

Amaziah is his name. I got to admit, he did warn me. Said he'd kill me if I went off prophesying and endangering his livelihood. He told me. But, I mean, he didn't have to non-metaphorically stab me in the back, though. I mean, c'mon—conduct unbecoming of a priest and all that. Just sayin'.

But nowadays—if you can say "now" or "days" in a place where time doesn't exist—nowadays we get on alright. We have breakfast every Tuesday. He's not sorry; but I'm not either. What I don't like most about him now is that he puts ketchup on his scrambled eggs. Nasty habit, if you ask me.

You get over most of the carbon-based stuff around here.

But back to my old stompin' ground: Nothin' but brackish, stinking water. Nothing green to speak of. Big washed-out gullies. That's the story of my life. Anywhere you find those things—which is pretty much everywhere on the planet—that's me; that's where I come from. That's where I am in my mind, much of the time, wherever I am now.

The Art of Prophecy

In case you're wondering, dead is a lot like alive. You see yourself as a self. You think. And then you do something because doing something appears to be the thing to do.

Anywhere you find some farmers scratching out an existence; find some shepherds surviving somehow; find some poor sot up a tree; find a prophet preaching in a YHWH–forsaken street; find a poet scratching away, trying to wrench meaning from images and words . . . anywhere you find those, you've found me.

Nothing to speak of. Yet, as with most humans & those who have been in that shape, I will speak. I will word on. Image on. It's that hope thing. Sometime, somehow, there must be something that can be said . . .. There must be some meaning that can be nailed down.

No. Ain't happened yet. But who knows?

Not that you're all that interested, I know. Really. I've been around, to say the least. You're not looking all that hard for a new way of thinking, now, are you?

& you're not searching for me.

You're searching for yourself. You're escaping your own Tekoa.

Who's looking for anyone besides themselves?

And furthermore, you only want to find easy and familiar things about yourself, am I right? Seriously?

& I'm not you. Really. I'm not. Or at least I perhaps wish I weren't.

But, since you're still here, I'll just up and tell you who I was when I was carbon–based: I was a carbon–based, decomposing shepherd. I was a dying pruner of sycamore trees. I was a slicer of figs who got stabbed in the back.

Let's Just Set the Scene Here

Not a path to fame & fortune, any of those things, huh? But did I say I ever dreamed of fame & fortune back when I was carbon-based?

Let me tell you who I was: Human. That's my excuse. That's my accusation. Ya wanna buy into that?

I mean, yes—as you shall learn, should you continue reading—there *is* some after-lifing—after a fashion—& even more after-living after that, it appears.

And there's that semi-timelessness thing going on—after a fashion—that comes with getting into scripture. Making it into scripture. The Bible, no less!

Yes. Even as a "minor prophet," there's some timelessness, after a fashion, in that. Until the world ends. Or the words end.

If any of that ever ends. You got me: I don't know.

Oh, but wait: if I haven't mentioned it yet, it ain't long off—that end of the world. (I have to throw that in, because it's expected of prophets. That "the end is near" thing. But, c'mon—is that a surprise? Have you read the news lately?)

You got yer bangs; you got yer whimpers. Who knows which will squeak in as the last one?

Anyhow, I'm slightly timeless, it appears, among the carbon-based, and that's called "fame." Not in a still-alive way but in a still kinda *known about* way. But not famous. Just infamous. Which is different. & I don't count as an upstanding, outstanding citizen. I'm not that either; never was. Nope. Lot's wife was . . . a pillar in her community . . . OK, you've heard that one before . . . . But, hey, she's good people too.

We do have some good comedians around here. Wherever "here" is.

And what about you? What's keeping you going on in your carbon-based format?

The Art of Prophecy

Me. I wasn't a pillar. Not a contributing member of society and all that.

Not a pillar; more of a basement. & I not rich. Not rich at all. Never was. I wasn't even a killer shepherd, come to that.

But here's the thing: even poor folks have insights. Think things. Get the combination on the safe of reality right, at times. Sometimes. Even poor folks. Even we uneducated, which is—I mean *was*—most of us. That's what I'm talking about. That's my main, bottom-line, YHWH's message: even poor folks see straight sometimes.

That's why I am—I mean I was—a major minor prophet.

Oh, and I know one other thing about your carbon-based world for sure:

Values cost.

Having them, I mean, has a cost. And paying ain't pretty.

So. There I was in a carbon-based form. And on long nights out in the desert; nights when there's nothing, nothing, & more nothing everywhere you look . . . on those kinds of nights, I'd hear a lion way off somewhere. A roar. A big, blood-curdling, roar.

Makes the hair on the back of your neck stand up. It does. Sends a cold shiver through you. Totally. Makes you see purple & taste copper & go blind for just a second or two. That roar. That's the school I went to—that roar.

You don't know where that lion is. You don't know if it's coming at you or going away. You don't know what that lion's about to kill. Is it aiming to kill one of your sheep? A snake? You? Who knows?

You don't know.

But what I've got to say is that when you hear that roar, you're awake. Wide awake. Aware. Listening. & that, my friends, is what a prophet is—somebody who just heard that roar.

Let's Just Set the Scene Here

Someone awake. Listening. Communicating.

Only it ain't a lion that's roared. It's YHWH Almighty, if that proper noun works for you. Call it what's good *for you*—nature; the dialectic; Baal. Something. & when YHWH roars, you're gonna lose more than a sheep & a little sleep.

Just sayin'.

That's what I'm talkin' about . . .

A Resume from the Other End of the Tracks

Oh, yeah, and that sitting out there among the stones listening to lions thing . . . my un–carbon–based bud John Cage says that having little or no purpose creates awareness. He says his purpose back when he was carbon-based was to remove purpose.

But, hell, when you're born poor, you're already half-way there. Am I right?

Starting something new. Something you have not done before. Like—oh, say—starting a career as a prophet. That's a leap ("of faith" may be stretching it, I often say to my bud Kierkegaard, but a leap).

No salary. No health insurance. No retirement account. No nothin'. All that's yours is debt and hard work.

& the very real possibility of massive blood loss down there in the stones of the street.

Starting a career as a real and true . . . no, check that . . . as an *hones*t prophet, I mean. Not one of the good–'ol–boy–guild. Not one to-the–manor-born set. Not one of the yes–sayers, fake–seers, ersatz–lap-dog–yea–ers in the employ of the power. In the employ of the parasites that suck the blood of the poor. If you get my drift . . .

(Yes, prophecy is about politics. But then everything is, come to that, no? And, to repeat, values cost. Are costly.)

A Resume from the Other End of the Tracks

Real prophet. Not something to put on the resume. But, then, "shepherd" or "sycamore pruner" don't look so good on there either, now do they?

Can you say "below base wage"?

The book called "Amos" says this about me: "He was one of the herdsmen of Tekoa." I didn't write that bit of my book—thanks for the clarification, there, editor of my book. As a resume, though, it ain't bad. Not a bad place to start as a prophet. Nowhere to go but up, after all.

Starting. But then all this stuff about paths & roads. Hell. Where I come from, there's no road or path. Just a general direction. Ask the folks around Tekoa about where to go from there, and they'll say, "Thataway, sort of." You'll see a worn spot here. Over there. Up there a ways. Worn down from hooves & bare feet. No connections, though. No way from here to there except by a sort of generally heading . . . thataway.

Consequently, as a consequence, we shepherds develop quite a nose for direction. General direction. & we get accustomed to not knowing quite which way. Or how much farther. Or further even. Just thataway. & if that-away doesn't work . . . well, there's always that–other–way.

Works just as well, that–other–way. How's that for a line on the resume?

> So, when I was clear on the call—
> clear on the sound that
> bound 'n' gagged justice makes—
> when I had that part;
>
> it was just sort of a thataway order
> that I got about where to go. North.
> Order from the Big Guy in the Sky
> who I haven't met yet and now
> I'm thinking that's not likely. (Nobody
> 'round here has met The Guy.)
>
> Anyway, something or somebody or
> maybe nobody told me "Go thataway.
> Northward. Where the big kingdom was.

The Art of Prophecy

Thataway, where the fattest parasites
attached themselves. Where the high
'n' mighty sat, attached, sucking

our blood. Thataway where a new
Pharaoh always sits, looking to lion
us all up like so many lamed

sheep.

That kind of call. That kind of resume.

Ya Hear Things

You hear things when ya listen.
(What is it anybody ever needs to know
before heading thataway?)

You hear things, herding sheep.
City folks may not think so, but you do.

I mean, you hear things besides lions roaring & sheep
   ... well ...
I'll talk about them some other time, the sheep.

You hear things from the outside world.
I mean, the bigger world where people
really do have roads that look like straight lines,
roads that look like they're going somewhere
in some kind of precise & serious way.
Those paved kinds of roads.

That kind of world. Bigger.

I heard about Assyria.
Crouching. Waiting.
I heard about Egypt.

Empires ...

They empire, don't they?
Which means they're out

The Art of Prophecy

to expand.

& expand.
& . . .

A shepherd & sycamore pruner can get that picture.

But the rich & the richer?
Not so much. Always they think
they can blood suck & buy
their way out.

We shepherds. Well.
Tight–spots–are–us.
We don't buy ways out, though.
Not shepherds.
Not sycamore pruners.
No money. No credit.

A tight spot just gets tighter.

When we hear things,
out in the desert,
we hear them as stark as
the rocks under our feet,
stones ringing, with
a little iron mixed in.

Assyria rising. The rich & the powerful
(let's just call 'em shepherds of the people
for this metaphor, shall we?), the powerful
& the rich drinkin' & yuckin' it up

while they suck the blood of the people.
While Assyria empired all over the place

—crouching. Growing.

You hear things when you're a shepherd.

Ya Hear Things

You really hear 'em & understand what's up:

Some good conversationalists to have a pint with.
South of the
North Pole,
it's all evil;
North of the
South Pole,
it's all good.

Like I've mentioned, I have some buddies I talk with here in this other-side-of-somewhere. Some good conversationalists to have a pint with. Brother Michel Foucault is one of my pub buddies. He says, "Truth is a thing of that world, produced only by virtue of multiple forms of constraint."

That Brother Michel. He don't like the way power works among some primates back in the carbon-based world.

He's good folk to have a pint with.

Just the Facts

According to *2nd Kings*:

> In the fifteenth year of Amaziah the son of Joash, king of Judah, Jeroboam, the son of Joash king of Israel, began to reign in Samaria, and reigned forty and one years.
> And he did that which was evil in the sight of the L-RD: he departed not from all the sins of Jeroboam the son of Nebat, who made Israel to sin.
> He restored the coast of Israel from the entering of Hamath unto the sea of the plain, according to the word of the L-RD G-D of Israel, which he spake by the hand of his servant Jonah, the son of Amittai, the prophet, which was of Gathhepher. (14:23–25 King James Version)

Get all that? I don't either. So Jeroboam II followed Jeroboam I, who was a good fighter but not much in the way of YHWH-following.

Jeroboam II is the guy I'm after when I head that–a–way north.

More on the Nothing of Silence

As I said, the one thing you learn in the desert night is silence. You develop one of those intimate relationships with silence. Roaring, deafening silence. Makes some tell stories. Makes some sing songs. Makes some hear things. Makes some as batty as loons. If you can sit with it, though. If you can trust it long enough to hear past the roar. The fear. Then. Then it speaks, that silence. It speaks a language that's beyond human striving. Way out there, beyond ego.

What silence says is not in words but in experience itself. Feeling. Doing. Experiencing.

Because the words of the heart are not words. Nor pictures, as in the mind. The silence speaks experience itself. That is the mystical experience. The unspeakable that so many images and words get spent on.

But always, it remains only silence, if by "only" you mean "everything." And by "silence" you mean all meaning.

> Yet it's always out there, in plain sight.
>
> Brother David said it this way—
>
>> I bless YHWH who counsels me;
>>   & in the night
>> my heart instructs me. (Psalms 16:7)

Which is which, Davey-Boy? It's one of the which-es or the other. Who's doing the counseling, Davy-Boy? Who's doing the instruction? Who's talking, YHWH or your heart? What the heck is the difference?

Ain't no difference.

At that moment, "the divine," the Other, the Not-Me, the Every-Thing-Is-Me, the inner-voice that has no outer, remains a mystery but becomes a deep experience.

Becomes experience itself.

Sister Catherine of Genoa, back when she was a carbon-based creature, shouted this in the streets: "My deepest me is G-D!"

She's good people to have a pint with, too. When you get here, wherever "here" is, put Sis Catherine on your dance card. (But, like me, she don't really dance.)

Being Nearly Timeless
(& Being & Time, Take 1)

Sure, being nearly timeless or close-to-immortal looks good from the outside, but it has its drawbacks, believe you me.

Seriously.

Sure, it's nice to know I was as right as rain; that my prophecies came true. Unlike my brother Jonah. Poor guy—dig that gourd that keeps growing, dude! So sorry everybody thinks you got grokked by a whale! Good story. Bad for the ol' takin' this serious thing.

No, seriously, it's nice to know that I even wrote some zingers that people remember—which I will remind you of in a bit, trust me! Gotta love them zingers when they come to ya!

It's nice to know that I made the cut; that I'm one of the Twelve Minor Prophets, & a major minor prophet at that.

Yet, to be timeless in a carbon-based way is to be old. Not as in arthritis old but as in brain old. Thinking old. The too many stories repeated too many times kind of old.

Because, you see, in addition to knowing all I've mentioned, I also know that it all—all I did back in my carbon-based days—didn't amount to a hill of beans. I mean, predicting the decimation of a nation?—so what's new?

The Art of Prophecy

There's a nation. You tell 'em decimation is on the way. Face it: you can't be wrong.

Besides, I didn't even get a leviathan in my story. Ever seen a children's book about me? Uh. No!

> Saying a nation
> will end in war
>
> is like saying
>
> a rabid dog will
> end up dead.

Prophecy like that is just shootin' fish in a barrel.

I'm that kind of old.

I know that I didn't manage to usher in the Day of YHWH, the Realm of YHWH, the Beloved Community, the Promised Land, or what-have-you. Justice-ville. Nope. Didn't happen.

Nothin'.

So, what's new?

No one else has ushered them in either.

I'm that kind of nearly timeless. The un-dead kind. I mean, you know . . . death is a carbon-thing.

Do you know what you learn, being nearly timeless in a non-carbon sort of way? That things come & go. Come & go.

That's what you learn. Think you know that already? Tell me about it! You know that already. That's the darn tedious part! My bud the Buddha told everybody about that a long time ago.

Being Nearly Timeless (& Being & Time, Take 1)

Even before I left the sheep, I knew that it's all here one day and then hell-n-gone the next. I knew that before I bought the carbon farm. I didn't need to go to *Gay Paree* to learn that one. That's the problem with being nearly timeless or at least not in line for dying anymore. One of the problems.

Do you know what's new?

>Getting over yourself.

>Now that's new!
>That's unique.

>You know what's hard?
>Climbing out of your rut.

>Now that's hard.
>That's unique.

Do you know how often I see those stories,
even being kinda, sorta timeless

in a not-exactly-dead sort of way?

Not so much.

Now I'm sort of timeless & I know that sort of thing, only more so! & more so is not unique. It's tiresome, as a matter of fact. It's just more of so, which nobody wants more of.

>How's that for being right? You're right.
>You're really, really right.

>& what does that get you?
>Timelessness. After a fashion.

>Timelessness.
>Of a sort.

The Art of Prophecy

    & what's that?
    More coming & going.
    More stories repeated more often.

    Only more so.

The next time I want more truth, I'll volunteer for a suicide prevention hotline, OK?

    I don't want it. It's not unique.

    That's one little drawback
    to being some sorta timeless.

P.S.:

OK, so I know that you & I know that time is just a construct—a construct that exists only in the imagination.

I know that my shepherd–monkey-mind is always chattering away & I should get into the now, which is really, actually, timeless. I know. Brother Buddha has me on a program. I'm on my way to the story outside of story, but I ain't there yet. Right now, I'm in a pub with my bro Yeats. Great guy to talk poetry with. He knows I go back & forth on the prophet & the poet thing & the difference between.

Know what my bro says?

    We make out of the quarrel with others, rhetoric,
    but of the quarrel with ourselves, poetry.

Yeah, have a pint with us, when you get here. It's as good a time as any in town . . . wherever it is we are.

Keep Your Trap Shut

Yes, if you want to be a prophet or a poet or both you've got to open your ears & be free from your own agenda. Your own propaganda. That's the starting line: zero. Meaning as few assumptions as possible.

I didn't think I *had* an agenda before I left the desert. I just wanted to survive as a shepherd. I wanted—if "want" even makes sense when you haven't thought about it— I wanted to stay down on the farm; I didn't have any interest in seeing *Gay Paree*. But that kind of no-agenda is an agenda. & it's about safety, huh? Am I right?

I had an . . . insight . . . & my agenda changed. That's what so-called mystical experiences are for. Or rather, what they do for you.

On my little walk from the desert hillside to the big city, the agenda of agendas presented itself. It got all "meta."

For we primates, the mind plays tricks & the ego ambushes along the way.

Brother Jonah fell into the trap. Sure, he obeyed his marching orders from the Great Beyond in his head. Then, lo & behold, the people repented. YHWH didn't smite them. Jonah felt aggrieved. His agenda called for the smiting, not for the repentance. His success made him a big loser in his prophetic adventure.

Makes no sense, am I right?

> Agendas never do.
> Take over the world?

The Art of Prophecy

Gain fame & fortune?

Sleep with this person or that?
Become a prophet or a saint?
What the hell for?

You've got to be free from your own agenda. Call it enlightened self-interest, in that agendas bring grief, and the agenda of no-agenda is pretty darn comfortable.

In worlds created by ego, the only opposite of an agenda appears to be passivity. However, in the spiritual world (the real one, I mean), there is only the ego-world of delusion & the liberated world of spirit, of creativity. Of letting what happens happen according to the flow of the universe, if you will. The Way of the Way, as the Brothers Lao-zis call it.

> We speak few words by nature—
> High winds do not last the whole
> Morning; a deluge does not pour
> All day. Why? Because even heaven
> & earth cannot stay violent long.
>
> When we make The Way our study
> Those pursuing it agree with us,
> & those practicing it agree with us,
> & even those failing to live up
> To their attempts agree with us.
>
> When we make The Way our study,
> Those attempting to practice it
> Agree with us, & those attempting
> To pursue it agree with us, &
> Even those failing to attempt it
>
> Agree with us.
>
> But when we stop
> Our own attempts,
> All others lose faith in us. (*Daodejing* 23)

Darn those collective brothers history calls Laozi. They nail it. Sometimes, even now, even non-carbon-based as I am, their success gets my ego-agenda in a wad!

Packing for the Trip

Having been outside of time for a long non-time, I have concluded (but no, there's never a conclusion, really, when we're being honest & nearly or entirely outside of time) that human beings do well to pack some variation on those classic three questions in our luggage for the long haul (helps clarify the agenda of the agendas):

What's real?

What's a human being, given what's real?

What should I do, given what's real and being a human being?

Those are the questions. Don't leave home without 'em. (& don't stay home without 'em, come to that!)

Each big-little carbon-based creature we call human must find the answers, or swim in the dark. Or buy somebody else's bull hockey.

It's difficult, leading that examined life, yes. Yet, if you're working on these three little koans, every story you hear will be some answer to the questions. (Keeping in mind that stories are necessarily creatures of the past & therefore work only partially in informing the present—the now—ya know.)

Ever noticed how you can't talk about much without talkin' about time?

For me, the desert was real. "Real" being something out to kill me. In that real desert were stories of a YHWH who was non-carbon-based and lived

Packing for the Trip

on a mountain dreaming of justice for all the carbon-based creatures. But it was a dream, that dream of YHWH.

And we carbon-based creatures—we don't need a dream. We need real.

& poverty. Poverty was real for me. Not the kind of poverty where you sit around & sob that you don't have a boat or a beach house or the latest lemming sort of thing. The kind of poverty where you're ashamed to be seen by rich folks. Afraid to be heard by rich folks. And you ain't got nothin'. That kind of poverty.

& in those stories of YHWH on a mountain;
& in that feeling that there was something out there
that wanted justice for everything in this world—there
I found what I should do as a human being
given what was real for me.

Given that I planned on saying my say, whatever.
Damn the thrown stones and the knives in the back.

That was my now. Built on stories that I had been told; built on stories I told myself.

For me, being human in that moment meant working for justice for everything—people, sheep, lions, stones—in that very real carbon-based world.

Ergo & Shazam—I had to put on my big-boy sandals & get to work for justice.

Cause & Effect—That's Where It's All At!

> We shepherds. We get
> the concept of cause
> & effect. Or, more proper,
> we know what kind of
> manure comes up
> when some manure
>
> goes down.

The problem for us prophets is that when you know—exactly—what's up & what's going to go down because it always does, you've got to say your truth, because, you know, the end is always near. Always. All the time.

Par exemple:

Two people walking together? Guess what—they've met.

"*Ergo sum*," ya know. It's in the definition of 'together" and "met."

Lion roars—it's about to jump on something.

(A lion growls—that's different. Means they've caught themselves something and don't plan on letting it go.)

It's all *ergo sum*.

Par exemple:

Cause & Effect—That's Where It's All At!

Ever see a bird trapped unless she's in a net?
(k, k, so I lived before plate glass windows!)

Ever see a trap tripped without something trippin' it?

Ever hear the warning siren & no one's lookin' scared?

That's the way I logic-ed with people. Cause & effect. *Ergo sum* stuff.

It's ef-fin logic. It's how I wrote—well, dictated, k? It's how I thought out loud when I was carbon-based.

Sure, in my time everybody thought some g-d or other did everything. *Ergo sum*, ya work with that. You ask a simple question: "Does a disaster happen & some g-d or other didn't do it?"

Seriously—is it always about one g-d or another?

If you get to the *QED* on that one, then it's all set up—you just gotta describe the disaster in compelling detail, ya know? Where would the End of the World be without compelling visuals?

Lion roars, there's fear.
YHWH speaks, it's prophesy!

A shepherd out there in the outback, way beyond help. A shepherd like me.

I learned cause & effect. I got at the *ergo sum*. I could see that when some manure comes up, other manure's gonna come down.

Don't think a dark, dark night won't talk to you.

Oh, yes, it will.

Ya hear that there lion?

I've got some *par exemples* for you . . .

Whinin' Like Habakkuk

Not to toot my own clarinet, but I didn't whine about my call. My vocation. My . . . vocalization.

I didn't do any of that "why me?" malarkey.

&, again, not to toot my own oboe, but neither did I wait around askin' "why?"

Yeah, the Auschwitz gate got it right—There's no 'why.'

Never is.

Not to toot my own French horn, but I think I'm being objective when I say I'm a more major minor prophet than Habakkuk ever was. Listen to him whine:

> O, YHWH, how long shall I cry & you won't hear?
> I cry out to you about the violence, & you don't stop it!
> Why have you shown me wrongdoing
> & caused me to see grievance?
> Spoiling & violence are before my eyes
> & those who cause strife & contention.
> The wicked have hamstrung the righteous.
> & the law is slack & judgment never happens.

Now, I'm just sayin'! He's still so ticked that he got all inconvenienced by his vo-cation that he won't even talk about it. I've invited him for coffee. Dude just sits there going on.

Whinin' Like Habakkuk

Brother Luke, on the other hand. He's so cool. Makes me happy Christianity came along so that we could get jumbled together in those sacred, holy, moldy pages everybody calls the Holy-By-Bil & would rather get wrong.

Now, Brother Luke, he don't whine. He's got all that education. He's got that literary-allusion thing goin' on.

Makes me wonder why my *ergo sum*s & *par exemple*s had to be straight out of the manure & the stones. Don't get me wrong—I ain't whinin' like you-know-who. I'm just sayin'.

Why do some of us find our voices in the finest books & conversations, & some of us have to speak our truths out of the bare, dry bones and stones of poverty & sun?

Why. Why. Why.

Why couldn't I have said it like Brother Luke, clear & elegant:

> He has brought down
> the powerful from their thrones,
> & lifted up the weak;
> he has filled the hungry
> with good things,
> & sent the rich away empty. (1:52–53)

OK, I get it—there never is a *why*. But there always is a *because*, now ain't there?

Let's look at it this way—everywhere you are, always that's where you are,

> Headed for the Lucky 7 Motel
> in some Texas or other.
> Or you're not. Odds on . . .
> You're not. But you are
>
> somewhere.

The Art of Prophecy

Ask Sister Joan D'Arc, speaking of *par examples* & the peasantry & all. She'll tell you: Getting to the place of speaking truth is a costly little process. Your whole darn dirt–poor domestic servant gene pool is going to add up to the truth you tell. & when you're comin' from there, ain't nobody gonna listen. You're gonna get yer bum fried.

Nope. Truth is just too hard to tell. And a damn sight harder to hear.

& for some of us—when we speak our truth on our very own creaky little soap box—well, agricultural metaphors will be heard!.

"Habbukkuk, buddy," I tell him, "Brother Donatello did you a statue." Sure, it don't look anything like you, but it ain't a shabby thing to have your name all over a Donatello. All I got was a Dore woodcut." (But I'm not whinin'.)

Have some coffee, dude!

Hunk a Burnin' Vo-cation

Major major prophet Brother Jeremiah felt it this way—

> O, YHWH, you enticed me,
> & I was seduced; you
> overpowered me,
> & you had your way.
>
> I'm a joke all the time;
> everyone mocks me because
> whenever I open my mouth,
> I shout, "Violence & destruction!"
>
> The word of YHWH has become for me
> a reproach & derision all day long.
>
> Sometimes I say to myself,
> "I will not speak the message I hear.
> I will not be YHWH's messenger any more."
>
> Then, the message burns
> like a fire in the marrow
> of my bones.
>
> I grow weary of trying
> to hold it in; I just
> can't keep from speaking.
>
> I hear the intrigue whispered against me.
> They say, "Come on, let's show him up!"
>
> All my so-called friends watch for

> me to stumble. They say, "He'll slip up,
> then we'll show him." (Jeremiah 20:7–10)

OK. There's some whinin' there. You can get down about your call & do the whole "why me?" thing. But you gotta say, Hey, Brother Jeremiah, get on with it! It's all kinds of nice to be all literary and metaphorical and all. Yez . . .

But, Jerry, you gotta get on with it!"

Got to Samaria & What Did I See? (Part I.)

Got to Samaria
& what did I see?

Just piles & piles
of vanity!

Got to Samaria
& what did I say?

"They trample the
heads of the poor,"
that's what I said,

"into the dust &

shove the meek
out of the way."
Full stop.

Here, After My Karmic Breakdown

Predictability is so damn predictable.
But maybe I can say that now only
because I've had a karmic breakdown.

My meltdown. I've had a lot of time to
think about smiting & righteousness

& the rich & their sandals
in the faces of the poor
& all that business

& how the pricks
that get kicked against
kick back & the kicked–
back get pricked.

Like the sands
of the desert,
greed goes
on & on.

No. Check that—
there's more greed
than there is sand.

Like the rocks,
injustice
rolls on.

Here, After My Karmic Breakdown

Finite, sure.
I suppose,

yet so endless
as to be nearly so.
On & on, some
things don't change;

'round & around.
Some of my conclusions
were not from agricultural
metaphors & their base in
the seasons of sun & moon.
So very little
new under the sun . . .

But that's another book
for another day.

Still, now, even today,
in carbon–based land
you don't run
a horse on solid rock.
Still, now, you don't
plow the sea with oxen.
See how nearly
timelessly
I wrote?

Some things are constant,
nearly. Things like change.

Brother Heraclitus is so
always right on that one.

Everything remains vanity.
Brother Queholet
is always right
on that one.

The Art of Prophecy

Even Brother Buddha's
shot at extinguishing vanity
is . . . well . . .
a bad snuff film.
No Nirvana neither.

You get the idea.
Sometimes it's depressing
after you've had
a karmic breakdown.

But me. I've always
wanted to see the
truth, whatever that
is, as clearly as clear
can be through
carbon–based eyes.

In that regard, it's
no better here.

Away Out That Way

    I got to Samaria & what did I see? Inequality!
    I got to Samaria & I stood my ground.
    I watched the goings on all 'round.

    Oh, yeah. Everything was in place.
    Done up right, according to tradition.
    Just what the priests had ordered,
    right & proper & turned the right
    direction, underwriting
    the rights of the rich.
    This was a temple to YHWH.

    Beaten like a bad dog
    by priests of the realm.

    That's what I saw.
    And here's what I say:
    any orthodoxy you see,
    burn it down!

Ol' Brother Luke doesn't want to tell me why he wrote his little Christmas tale the way he did. Angels singing "hallelujah!" Where'd he get that stuff?

Oh, man! Who wouldn't want to have written that? But how did a city boy know what it feels like, way out in the utter dark?

He's a cagy guy, that Brother Luke. Even after a couple of pints.

The Art of Prophecy

It would be the best kind of high—a flashy angel choir singing "peace on earth" & "hallelujah" & all. I couldn't even have imagined that in some sort of crazy wish-fulfillment dream.

> All I got was a lion's roar.
> (But I ain't whinin' like Habakkuk!)
> Oh, YHWH, you're good that way...
> Passing things like talent out
> all arbitrary like, I mean.

Brother Luke's good people, really. You just have to understand the way educated folks can be, bless 'em.

Imagine. Writing a whole darn book & never saying what you really think. Just... hinting. Or whatever people like Luke with a literary, educated, turn would call it. "Alluding to." Saying how poor folks & women are more turned-on & tuned-in to the sacred.

That's rich! That's stickin' it to the power. Good work, Luke, 'ol man. It ain't true, but I sure do wish it were.

> Stuff & bother. I suppose somewhere—
> deep down somewhere—I wish I could
> have got 'ol Luke-boy's education
> & ways with them words.
>
> Just tryin' to be honest.
> Somewhere down there I've
> got some whine goin' on.
> But YHWH knows... something.
> Provides... Something.
> Even if YHWH's all
> up in our heads.
>
> (See: I'm not whinin' like Habakkuk!)
>
> But that's the difference:
> Bein' a shepherd & writin'
> about 'em in some

Away Out That Way

metaphorical sort of way.

When you live in the sheep shit,
you don't allude, ya know?
You know what it smells like.

You don't pull no punches
when you walk around
with a knife in your hand
cuttin' the fruit on sycamore trees
just to ripen 'em up enough
to make 'em so folks can eat 'em.

"Sycamore pruner."
Makes me sound like I was out
in somebody's garden trimming
trees for an extra buck.

No. Out in the hedgerows
cutting the damnedest
poorest excuse for a fig–like
something that there is.

Just to sell something to
poor folks so that they feel
like they've eaten something
like the rich folks, who buy
figs as an afterthought.

Boy, howdy.

Got to Samaria & What Did I See? (II.)

Got to Samaria &
what did I see?

Say it with me:
in–equ–al–ity.

So what's new?
Nothin's new.

Say it with me—
The rich are just
out there
suckin' blood.

Say it with me,
what is all we
see?

in–equ–al–ity.

No, really: When I got to Samaria, what do you think I saw?

King Jeroboam the Second
doin' everything right . . .
politically speaking. &
politics are about results,

am I right? Yep.

Got to Samaria & What Did I See? (II.)

'Ol Second was gettin' results,
that Jeroboam Two.

He'd dodged into the space between the egos in Assyria & the egos in Egypt & played 'em off against each other.

He took back land his goofy family had lost in the days since Solomon.

He made nice with little Judah to the south.
(Once, later, he even said I could say my piece.)

When I climbed Samaria's seriously scenic hillside, everything was hunky dory for good 'ol Jeroboam II.

    So what do you think I saw?

    I'd been hearing stories along the way:
    Children bought & sold.

    Property of the poor foreclosed.
    Land swindled from farmers.

    A farmer's daughter traded
    for a pair of sandals because

    her father needed sandals
    for work. You know what I saw.

    The usual thing
    is what I saw.
    What happens
    every–damn–day.

    Human nature ever is
    the same. Darn primates,
    heads so easy to turn
    with a promise of more.

    You know what I saw.

The Art of Prophecy

You see it.

You don't have to be
outside of time—or even
a major minor prophet
to know how it was.

So what did I do? Well, sir,
I had my big–boy sandals on.
I marched right up the hill
& straight to the temple

(because you know
& I know that
religion is always
right there ready to say
the rich have the right
to do as they like)

& what did I see?
You know what I saw.

Well, OK, you don't know
particulars.

So, I'll say I saw an old custom: somebody borrows money for the day; he takes off his coat & leaves it at the altar for pawn. That evening, he pays back the money & picks up the coat. It's a system that works, because who's going to go without his coat in a desert night if he doesn't have to?

Money gets borrowed; debts get paid. That one is an old particular, but the outcome's the same. & you know how it was—the coats stacked up. Because the poor just get poorer.

When I went up the hill & into the temple, what did I see?

    Temple prostitutes swilling wine,
    passed out drunk on piles of coats.

Got to Samaria & What Did I See? (II.)

Coats stolen by wile & law.
Coats stolen from honest folks

tricked out of their loans & coats.
Coats off the backs

of the poor, on
their way to enrich

the rich & the priests.

That's what I saw.

Then there was the little matter of the temple prostitutes themselves. Children. Kids.

Now, I'd heard about that. If you're thinkin' with your pocketbook, it's a deal, after all. Sex: The best way to keep a temple in fine fettle & keep 'em comin' in. Just turn your temple into a brothel. Just say it's sacred to pay for sex there. Keeps 'em comin'. Keeps the Building & Grounds Committee happy & the temple assets liquid & flowin'. It's a fine, workable idea.

When you're thinkin' with your pocketbook.

Fine idea. Except, well, that it's evil.

What did I see? I saw, when I marched up that hill into that temple with my big-boy sandals on, a father & a son had paid for the same girl. There on that pile of stolen coats.

My jaw dropped. I just stared. The father saw me watching. "You want a piece of this, get in line," he said.

"Stinking farmer wouldn't have the money!" the son said.

"& why might that be, ya think?" I said.

O, my brother James said it right a whole lot later in time,

The Art of Prophecy

>Consider this: the wages of the laborers
>who harvested your fields,
>you kept back by fraud;
>the laborers cry out, & that cry
>has reached the ears of YHWH. (5:4)

"Ooop, I tripped," some slobbering drunk said, falling into me & almost knocking me down.

>I got to Samaria & what did I see? Inequality.

>I got to Samaria & I stood my ground.
>I watched the goings on.

>Oh, yeah. Everything was in place.
>Done up right, according to tradition.
>Just what the priests had ordered,
>right & proper & turned the right
>direction, underwriting
>the rights of the rich.
>This was a temple to YHWH.

>That's what I saw.
>Yet. Yet . . .

So, I took myself a long drink of water, & I said this, nice & loud:

>This is what YHWH says:

>For three crimes of Israel,
>& for four, I will not turn away
>punishment
>because you enslaved
>debtors for silver,
>& sold the poor for sandals—

>Chasing after the dust
>of the earth,
>you push the weak away
>& trample on
>the heads of the poor.

Got to Samaria & What Did I See? (II.)

I woke up the next morning with a bad lump on my head.

All Wisdom, All the Time

    Trees & water;
      desert & sun;

    even the worms,
      the flies; even
      the mosquito's

    buzz teaches

    wisdom to
      the wise, to

    the listeners.
    Every creeping

    thing. Every form
      a hint of all.

    Trees & water;
      desert & sun,

    even the rocks
      & oxen, even
      two walking

    together teach
      wisdom to
      the wise,

All Wisdom, All the Time

to those
  listening.

Listen.

Pride of Place

Was I the first of a new breed of prophet—the outside & the against, the anti-status, the anti-quo? The anti-he-ro? Was I the first to talk about a "Day of the L–RD"? The first to write my own book? (OK, "dictate." Back off!)

>Could be. Scholars with educations say so.
>Who knows?
>
>When you're as old as I am—
>if old means anything here—
>& very outside of time,
>the twinkle of the frost on a leaf
>interests more considerably
>than who did what when.
>Than who won any wars
>or ruled any empires.
>
>Darn primates & their "first!" this,
>"biggest!" that, "primo!" the other thing.
>
>Get this joke: I couldn't write a friggin' word!
>Illiterate in my carbon-based form, children.
>I didn't "write" nothin'. But speakin' words.
>That I could do, after my agricultural manner.
>
>Still and all . . .
>
>I heard the lion's roar.

Pride of Place

I headed north to
the two places,
the two boot heels—hold it—
make that " two sandals"—
holding the people down—

Samaria & Bethel.
Bethel & Samaria.
Heels holding
the people down.

I had some images in my head.
I had some poetic words I'd
   worked through as I walked.
I had my rage. I had my anguish.
I had my agra–metaphors.
I had my vision of the right.
I had my authority in
"thus says the L–RD."

I knew that sometimes people
look to be on top of the world
when they're really in the . . .

fecal matter.

   We always are
   both &. We are

because that is
   the way of humanity

   itself. Consciousness
itself. Reality itself.

Darn primates.
Poor primates.

Poor, poor carbon.

The Art of Prophecy

If not you,
    who, prophet?

Embody It, Baby

1.

Facts, the stiff-necked beasts,
won't bow to abstraction.

(Well, to numbers, maybe,
but that's not where I'm at.)

Prophets split
the story line—crack
what we know so
that we may feel,
understand
in the heart.

Constructed religions.
Constructed governments.
Images, thoughts, feelings.

We've got to join in
with our own guts,

partners in creation
not prisoners, victims

of what money names real.
Creators, prophets, poets,

pray–ers outside con–
vention, outside

abstraction, feeling
into image–in–ation:

2.

There is something
outside our minds

mightier than we;
there is something

outside our minds
but not

outside us. Image–
ine that!

Embody that!

Mundus imaginalis,
"imagined world,"

realer than this one.
Oh, yes. Yes.

Shouting in the Street/Jostling

The Brothers Laozi nearly always say it best. They've just got that ethereal/*mysterioso* thing goin' on. "Name it & it goes away" & all that. It's all about context. I guess that's what they're drivin' at.

It's not that I didn't know, even in my time as a carbon-based creature, that shouting in the street wasn't the way to get across a message of peace & compassion. But who would have heard me, had I played a flute? Now, riding a water buffalo like that legend of Brother Laozi, that would have done the trick, if I'd had one of those. Water buffalo, I mean.

Ain't no water buffalo where I come from.

The way I see it, finally—justice & righteousness are about peace. Peace is always the answer to any social or religious question. The question is how to get to the place that peace can operate. And I hope it goes without sayin' that the usual situation—rich boot—or sandal—on poor head—is not that place.

Way I see it, the Brothers Laozi still had that kind of top-down thing going on. As the universe, so the ruler, so the self, & all that.

I don't see that any ruler has ever been good. You don't hear any wise ruler talk from me. Or messiah talk. Or any of that Golden Age sheep manure. Nope. Brother Karl M. & me. We're together on the rule of the people stuff, though I don't think anybody should rule. Nobody's boot belongs on anybody's head. I've seen the problems. I've seen the sandals.

Both ways. It's anarchy all the way up; and all the way down.

The Art of Prophecy

So. Therefore ... Can any politics create peace? Always there is the human search for glory. A silly impulse, but natural in a primate. Always there is the human search for challenge, as Brother Dostoyevsky said so well. Or there is the human quest just to muck things up, as Brother Dostoyevsky also says so well.

Ergo and therefore, no: politics can never solve the problems that primates suffer.
Carbon–based creatures just ain't gonna stay airborne for very long.

There's a solid spiritual truth to it all:

Oppression oppresses the oppressor.

Go anarchy.

Talking, Back-to-the-Wall

So, you're planning on trying the prophet thing. Here's how you take in an audience, my dears:

"Tell the truth but tell it slant," as Sister Emily Dickinson put it. (No, Sister never did any busking or prophesying, but she sure could play the people, if you know what I mean.) Like Sister, I found somewhere along the path that I can't write—or think, rather—discursively. What I image-ine doesn't "dwell in possibility," as Sister ED says. Saying anything with a thesis just seems to me to be a hocus-pocus move. Half-truth.

So, the day after the bump on my head, I got up, put on my big-boy sandals, and I walked back into that temple & put my back to the wall & my shoulder to the wheel

I'd spent some time thinking about how to tell it slant, that truth thing.

Back to the wall, I sang out:

> This is what YHWH has to say:
>
> For three crimes of Damascus,
> & for four, I will not turn away
> punishment. No, for they
> threshed Gilead with tools of iron.
>
> I will send fire to the house of Hazael
> that will destroy the stronghold at Ben-hadad.
>
> I will split the gates of Damascus

The Art of Prophecy

    & isolate the people
    & their leader.

    The people of Syria shall go
    into captivity in Kir, YHWH says.

Oh, you should have heard the cheers that went up when I'd finished that rant. (The dad and the son even stopped going at their new girl for a minute.) Our old enemy Syria punished. Hip, hip: three cheers for another nation's problems! Schadenfreude, ya know.

So, I kept at it:

    This is what YHWH says:

    For three crimes of Gaza,
    & for four, I will not turn away
    punishment because
    they carried captives into
    exile in Edom.

    I will send a fire to the wall of Gaza
    that will destroy its strongholds,
    & I will cut off
    the inhabitants from Ashdod & the one
    who holds the scepter of Ashkelon,

    & I will turn my hand against Ekron,
    & the remnant of the Philistines shall perish,
    YHWH says.

Loud cheers. (The girl took a potty break.) I had 'em now. Schadenfreude sells.

    This is what YHWH says:

    For three crimes of Tyre,
    & for four, I will not turn away
    punishment because they exiled
    whole towns to Edom,
    breaking their promises.

Talking, Back-to-the-Wall

> I will send a fire to the wall of Tyre
> that will destroy their stronghold.

"Three cheers for what the good YHWH has to say!" somebody yelled.

Three cheers for schadenfreude, ya know . . . I kept on:

> This is what YHWH says:
>
> For three crimes of Edom,
> & for four, I will not turn away
> punishment because they pursued
> their kindred with the sword,
> throwing away all pity,
> & their anger tore & tore,
> their wrath going on & on.
>
> So I will send a fire on Teman
> that will destroy the walls of Bozrah.

"Go! Go! Go! Go!" the crowd chanted. (I noticed that the girl wasn't coming back.)

Now hear this: You can't miss when you're appealing to prejudice. & that apocalypse stuff. People eat that up. Schadenfreude. People eat it up like greasy freedom fries. I kept at it:

> This is what YHWH says:
>
> For three crimes of the children of Ammon,
> & for four, I will not turn away
> punishment because
> they have ripped apart
> the pregnant women of Gilead
> merely to expand their borders.
>
> So I will build a fire on the walls of Rabbah,
> & it will destroy their protection when
> the shouting comes, in the day of battle,

The Art of Prophecy

>   when the tempest hits,
>   in the day of the whirlwind.
>
>   Then their king will go into captivity,
>   he & all their ruling class, YHWH says.

"Yes! Yes! Put it to 'em farm boy!"

So much for schadenfreude. I hit 'em with the coup–de–kicker, a little repeat of the truth from the day before. A little parade rain for the home team:

>   This is what YHWH says:
>
>   For three crimes of Israel,
>   & for four, I will not turn away
>   punishment. Because you sold
>   the righteous for silver,
>   & the poor for sandals—
>
>   Yes, you chased profit, the dust
>   of the earth, & you trampled
>   the heads of the poor
>
>   & shoved the meek
>   out of your way.

So Many Ways to Say . . .

One of those good 'ol fashioned Proverbs said it best,

> Wisdom shouts in the street;
> In the squares she preaches.
>
> At the busiest corner she proclaims;
> At the entrance of the city gates
>
> She speaks: "How long, O, simple ones,
> How long will you love being simple?" (1: 20–30)

You ask me, & I'm gonna say, Sure, I'm envious of those other places, other traditions, where street corners, soapboxes, & screaming ain't necessary.

I think of Brother Tenryu, Zen guy, who could hold up one finger & get at it all—everything that needed saying—get it all across. People heard him. Heard his finger, I mean.

Why did I have to waste so much sweat & breath, so much spittle & blood, in the desert, among violent & ignorant people, saying my truth?

Why, why, why? (But, Bro Habbakuk, look–see—I ain't whinin'.)

Just think of what might have been, if we desert people could have heard the whole thing out of the voice of one finger. If we could have heard the sermon of one flower, like the one Brother Buddha held up.

> One flower for a scripture.
> One flower & a smile . . .

The Art of Prophecy

& the communication's done.
'Nuff said.

Think about it. What might have been. No Sodom. No Gomorrah. No West Bank yah–yah–yahs. But there are no diamonds in the desert, except those shipped in. No pearls.

No. We. We dry-climate folk. We're about killing. About imperatives & slaughters. About not listening—to flowers; to shouts; to swords. All we hear or know is apocalypse.

We. In the desert . . . Today & every day under our pitiless sun . . . we want blood.

It's the sun does it, I suppose. The big, blue–black sky, that might be YWHA, I suppose.

Guaran-Damn-Teed

So, before I tell you the rest of that story, here's something I've been cogitatin' on: we humans—uh, you humans—take up so much time taking up time. Doing. Getting on it & off it & gettin' it done.

> That's the deal.
> But there's no deal.
> That's the deal.
> How often do we
>
> answer a straight question?
> How often do we ask one?
> Even of ourselves?

So, let's get down to it: Do I really . . . Really . . . Absolutely. Truly. Believe that YHWH told me those things?

Ah! There's the rub!

(If I could buy you another round, I would. But near-eternity doesn't have pockets 'n' everything's free.)

Depends on what you mean by "believe" & "YHWH."

No. Seriously. I'm bein' straight with you.

If you believe in YHWH, my nearly-timeless little mind thinks you next need to ask yourself what you think you're getting from your belief that YHWH exists.

The Art of Prophecy

Seriously.

Ask yourself: Do you need for "YHWH" to exist to underwrite & guaran–damn–tee what you learned to believe as a child? Or perhaps what you believe now with all your heart & mind? And, hey, those are not the same, are they?

Or do you need for "YHWH" to exist because you believe that "YHWH" exists?

&/or, do you believe, perhaps, that "YHWH" needs to exist to prevent a chaos you fear; or to guarantee that piety is rewarded; or wrongdoing punished?

&/or is it perhaps that you have always felt the existence of "YHWH," or have had an experience that convinced you that "YHWH" exists?

And there we go, off into subjectivity.

For me, during my carbon–based existence, I never questioned the existence of the "YHWH" I learned about as a child. & the "YHWHs" of other peoples, for that matter.

Furthermore, I came to believe that the "YHWH" I believed in under-wrote & guaran–damn–teed the message that I became convinced I needed to preach.

That's how it worked for me.

I'm being straight with you.

You can figure out how it works for you. The end point is conviction and action in a direction. How you get there, that's your problem.

So it all builds from there. Then, to be straight with you, I believed being alive was about *doing something*. Action.

Guaran-Damn-Teed

Good for a shepherd who is expected to work his life away, no? But when you hang out your shingle as a prophet, other rules begin to apply.

But, see, there you go. I could not have cared less about what anyone thought about my message, you know, inside their heads. As I saw it, if you've got your boot—er, sandal—on somebody's head, that's the problem.

The sandal on the head is the problem. What you're doing is the problem. Doesn't matter a tinker's damn whether you think you should have it there or not or if you think you're justified or not. It's just there. & having it there ain't never right.

Doesn't matter if you think "YHWH" or "YHWHs" told you to do it. Or profit & loss. Or your rights. Or democracy. See, that's where it gets tricky. I'm just bein' straight with you. It all gets tricky. Still, I think the thinkin' doesn't matter. It's what you're *doin'*.

Those other things just don't matter. Your religion. Your politics. Don't matter.

> The sandal in the face is the problem.
> The domination is the problem.
> The violence to the rights & wishes
> of another human being just like you
>
> is the problem.

This is another kind of belief than belief in YHWH.

Just bein' straight with you.

Now, go be straight with yourself.

'Nuff said.

Matters to the Whats-it-ites

Okee-dokey. Another thing I'll say about we human beings and those of us who have been human beings: we sure know how to hate on each other. Who the hell knows the difference between a Moabite & an Edomite?

Just sayin'.

Well, the Moabites & the Edomites for two, huh? & so off they'll run, hatin' on each other. For differences no one else can see.

People!

>If they're in the same family, they won't speak;
>if they're in the same neighborhood, they'll form gangs;
>if they're in the same city, they'll figure out the difference between
>>a Northside & Westside or
>>what-have-you &
>>backstab in the city council;
>
>if they're in the same country, they'll have themselves a bloody little civil war;
>if they're in different nations . . . war, war, war.
>
>We human beings, dang us, (I mean
>*you* human beings) will find a difference,
>from eye color to skin color to religion.
>I know!
>
>I used to be one of you!

Matters to the Whats–it–ites

War, war, war between
the We–Know–We're–Rights
& the Poppy–cock–ites.

Saying that we're just built that way,
or that it's always been thus,
amounts to just more bad behavior.

(You're not getting off said
hook that easy, you bloody
little primates.) But, see:
it takes a government
to really make people nasty.

& some thumbing
of our bloody little fingers
through our holy books

for excuses.
More bad behavior!

I told the truth in my little major minor prophetic book. I said that
YHWH told me to say this:

> Children of Israel,
> aren't you like the
> children of Ethiopia
>
> to me?
>
> Didn't I bring you
> up to Israel, out
> of the land of Egypt?
>
> & the Philistines
> from Caphtor,
> & the Syrians
> from Kir?

There, take that, all you chosen people. Sure, you're *all* chosen. Get over it.

Now, make something of yourselves besides bloody little butchers.

True Confession

OK. True confession: I didn't write that last bit about the Ethiopians & the Syrians & the Philistines.

I didn't write all of my book. I'm a little less an author or a prophet, or a poet for that matter, than my portfolio might suggest . . .

(Uh. Well, actually, I was illiterate. But, hey, what can you do? Earns me my proletarian spurs, no?)

Still, don't I get some credit, since those good words appear in my major minor prophet book? Let's say that I inspired those words with my words, even though it happened to be somebody a little after my carbon–based–demise who formed the letters.

Go ahead: go on out in the street and say something so memorable that somebody will write it down. Just try it and see how difficult it is.

It was little 'ol major minor prophet me who inspired the words to conclude my major minor prophet book that got written down because I was so good at sayin' it right.

What could I do? After that big earthquake people thought I'd predicted, then forty years on when Israel actually fell, my words looked like gospel! Word. So, they started making copies. Then others jumped on my notoriety bandwagon to include some prophecy about Judah, the remaining bit.

What's a poor major minor prophet to do?

The Art of Prophecy

Seriously, I see my work as the inspiration, somebody latching onto my text & my name. I'm a muse. I like it. Prescient presaging, I think it should be called.

Prescient. Way ahead of its time. Today included. Your time 'n' all.

Sagish—sage-like, saying: We're all alike, we poor creatures of clay. Israel. Ethiopia. Egypt. Syria.

> Alike in our greed,
>   pride,
>   murderousness,
> & hope,
>
> you darn primates.
>
> Greed.
>   Anger.
>   Ignorance.

Just bein' unthinkingly human, am I right?

Yes, I'll take the credit for the additions. It's all good, except when, well, those so inspired mess it up.

Now, Brother Job, he's got something to kvetch about. I mean besides the potsherds & the sores & having his children killed. His whole darn story got messed up with additions & subtractions.

Me? The process left me lookin' good.

I'm Amos & I approve this message.

Those Big Scary Amorites

So.

The whole nearly-timeless and kinda timeless or so-so immortal thing works the other way too. Some things don't translate across the ages, shall we say. In my time, the Amorites were known & feared as giants, crazed herders without borders, houses, or culture. So, when I said that YHWH had delivered us from the Amorites, it meant something:

> & wasn't it I
> who brought you up
> out of Egypt,
>
> & led you forty years
> through the wilderness,
> to take the land of the Amorite?
>
> It was I who defeated
> the Amorites, who are
> as tall as the cedars,
>
> as strong as the oaks.
> I destroyed their fruit
> from above,
> their roots from below.

Yea! raw! YHWH!

I mean, you've gotta admit, "tall as cedars" & "strong as oaks" are pretty clever phrases, no? You get the size & strength thing there. & then the thing about "fruit from above" & "roots . . ." Pretty good, right? Sure, I

The Art of Prophecy

was playing to the cheap seats. Pushin' all the prejudice buttons. Still, nice images, no?

I mean, look at it this way: somebody's gotta invent the wheel before it can get re-invented, and somebody's gotta say the cliche before it becomes.

BTW, good 'ol John is way tired of all the Revelation and "fire and brimstone" stuff. John. He cringes a lot.

& then there's that brilliant little parataxis move that some of us poets like so well, slappin' in the twist on ungratefulness,

> I raised up your children as prophets,
> & your young to be Nazarites,
> separate & consecrated.
>
> Isn't this how it is,
> children of Israel?
>
> But you gave the Nazarites
> wine to drink;
> & told the prophets
> to shut their mouths.

Yeah, OK. So you had to be there to get that bit.

Thanks for Asking (a rant-ette)

Oh, imagine that! You didn't ask me about my mum.

That's how it is, isn't it? You're thinking, Hey, this former guy's a major minor prophet. He's nearly timeless in a sort-of time-based sort of way! He's got it all together. He ought to be on some kind of documentary about major minor prophets. He's like Mussolini or somebody.

Sure, he's famous. Hang him up by his heels.

Really. Admit it. That's what you think . . . That I was all kinds of ersatz and cardboard back in my carbon-based days. Admit it. That's what you think . . . .

A shadow play in a cardboard factory.

Admit it. You think that when you're a major minor prophet & have nearly achieved some kind of timelessness & even death & being rotted back to your constituent carbon bits—something about reality is going to call you out and make you all kinds of special. That you never even pissed or sweated.

You got another think comin', bub.

Being outside of time just means that you've watched generations of parents come and go.

Bouncing children grow old, you know. And then go to dust. All that carbon. Earth's the ultimate recycling plant, you know?

The Art of Prophecy

Don't get me started!

Thanks for askin'.

Not!

See, here's the thing—admit it—it hasn't occurred to you to ask me what I want for my birthday, now, has it? Admit it. I'm not on your Christmas card list. It just hasn't occurred to you to treat a major minor prophet-poet like a human being. Even a dead one.

Never does, see?

Alright, I'll just say it before you think I'm whinin' like Habakuk: that's the problem with humanity these days. I'm not sayin' it's ever been good. Used to be, you'd go off worshiping the Latest New Thing in the way of some golden calf or other. Now—well. Who needs newfangled YHWHs when you've got a new gizmo to get? When you've got the latest new thing & a line of credit for some more new gizmos?

I'm just sayin'. Empathy ain't us.

And, admit it, you didn't think to ask me about my birthday.

A Little *Zohar* Break

Deep Breath (*Zohar* 71:2)

All the universe
A single point,

The primeval
Thought

Hidden in plain
Sight, waiting

To be noticed,
To be thought.

The beginning
Of all will,

All thought.
Each point.

Each line
A start,

A door to
The mystery.

Got to Carry that Load

"Amos."

Amos, Amos. (The name means "carrying a load.")

Oh, I could start sending out invitations to my pity party over that one. I couldn't be "beloved." Or "shining one." Or even . . . .

Oh, no. Just good 'ol "carryin' a load."

What were my parents thinking? No, they didn't give me that name to be ironic. Mum & dad weren't socialists. They didn't see their lot as anything but YHWH-given & right in the hierarchical nature of things.

Some are born in the big city;
some shovel sheep shite.

Some are paupers; some are kings.
Some swill wine on ivory-studded beds.

Some freeze their asses off by a pitiful fire
out watching sheep. & let YHWH Almighty sort 'em out.

Oh, & some can make a silk purse out of a sow's ear. Like my poetry:

> Just as the shepherd pulls
> two legs, or a piece of an ear,
>
> from the mouth of a lion,

Got to Carry that Load

so will the children of Israel

be taken out,
a leg of a bed,
a piece of a couch.

Yeah, yes. Correct, it's wish fulfillment. It's class warfare in my own mind. But I couldn't've had the vision, you fat cattle, if you hadn't put me there!

"'Scuse me: I'm Amos, born to haul yer load." Look in my eyes. Seriously. See the hate.

Got to Samaria & What Did I See? (III.)

King Omri. King Ahab.
Queen Jezebel. Big time
once–wuzzes. There I was
   walking in the footsteps
   of Elijah, last of his kind;
   little 'ol me, first of mine.

I walked Samaria's streets
& it was all there,
the brutal & the lavish.
   Storied, mythical already.
   The lavish & the brutal.
   All underwritten, guaran–damn–teed
Kosher, by a corrupt temple
& the (backstabbing) priests in Bethel.

I put all my busker talent in one basket & let it out on a street corner:

   This is what YHWH says:

   Enemies shall encircle the land;
   enemies shall wring
   your strength from you,
   your high walls knocked down.

   This is what YHWH says:

   Just as the shepherd takes
   two legs or a piece of an ear
   out of the mouth of a lion,

Got to Samaria & What Did I See? (III.)

so shall the children of Israel—
those dwelling in Samaria
& Damascus—be found,

a corner of a bed,
a piece of a couch.

Hear & testify
in the house of Jacob,
YHWH says,
 L-RD of Hosts,

that on the day
that I shall return
the crimes of Israel
I shall also visit on

them, the altars of Bethel—

the horns of the altar
shall be cut off
& fall to the ground.

& I shall smite
the winter house
& the summer house;

& the houses of ivory
shall perish,
& the great houses

shall have an end,
YHWH says.

Sayin' It Straight

My bud Emil Cioran is not a vat a laughs on any day, but he says it like he sees it. Some has got rose colored glasses. Some has got flat black. And this is how he sees the job:

> To unmask them, to knock them off the pedestal they have hoisted themselves on, to hold them up to scorn is a campaign no one should remain indifferent to. For at any price we must keep those who have too clear a conscience from living and dying in peace.

Yeah! "At any price."

I said this:

> Alters and summer houses
> go together like enclosure
> and foreclosure, no?
>
> Let's just say it straight:
> that purity stuff; that
> incense & candle stuff—
> the bells 'n' smells—
>
> it's for the high-placed & the powerful.
> It's for the blood-sucking parasites
> deep 'n' comfy in the fur they're hidin' in.
>
> It's what priests do to keep being priests.
> Do to keep systems & buildings alive.

I don't know how to be more explicit:

> True religion is not about
> what you do to show holy.
>
> True religion is about
>
> caring for the oppressed,
> the depressed; the suppressed.

Couldn't be simpler. The first person to benefit from performing religious rites is the professional who gets paid to do religious rites.

The second is the person paying to give a sacred glow to whatever crimes makes the payola flow.

Third and last is you 'n' me.

Idolatry. Dogma. Institutionalization. Those are the biggies that kill genuine religious experience—

& you know what a system is? A systematic . . .

(Nope. Won't say.)

> When you're out in the middle of nowhere;
> out in the dark, the real dark;
> that's when you know what's out there,
> which is nothing. *Nada.*
>
> You feel *it*.
> & *it* don't fit
> into any temple,
> any system.
>
> Look at those stars when
> there's not even a candle
> to stab the darkness

The Art of Prophecy

for miles around.

That's when you know
what's out there.

The power. The emptiness.
The ain't–nothingness.

The forgetfulness. The forgottenness.

I don't suppose rich folks can ever feel that.
They never ride that far out on the pale horse.
Never that far out into utter, utter nothin'.

So, they write checks to priests.
And temples. And systems. See?

Sure, call me a class warrior.
Call me a Social Justice Warrior.
Whatever. You can't reach me.

SJW.

I'm invisible.
I ain't carbon
no more.

Idolatry Chant

My Yogi Brother Aurobindo says, "We must not raise any institution to the rank of a fetish. Doing so is simply becoming slaves to our own machinery."

Well done, brother. That never bowing to institutions thing.

>What are institutions?
>Human creations.
>
>What do they hurt?
>The human condition!
>
>What is bowing to human creations?
>I . . .
>
>I'll give you a few hints:
>
>I . . .
>Id . . .
>
>Id–o . . .
>Ido–lllll . . .
>
>You got it!
>I–dol–a–try!
>
>Say it with me:

The Art of Prophecy

Idolatry!
Idolatry!

Uh.
Um.
Don't do that,
that idolatry thing!

House of Israel, did you bring me
sacrifices & offerings in
the wilderness forty years?

(No? But I was there anyway?
Huh! says the L–RD.)

Yet, here you are, carrying
images of Moloch & your
Lord Sak'kuth, things
you made for yourselves.

Out of your own minds.
For this I will cause you
to go into captivity beyond

Damascus, says YHWH, whose
name is *The* L–RD of Hosts.

Full-Tilt Prophetic (*Amos* Chapter 4)

Now hear this,
you cows of Bashan,
living on Samaria's mountain,

you who oppress the poor,
who crush the needy,
who say to their husbands,

"Bring me something to drink!"

YHWH has sworn by
YHWH's own holiness,

saying, look: the day will come
when you will be taken away with hooks,
& your children with fishhooks.

You will escape through
holes in the walls, one cow
running after another—

YHWH says so.

Go ahead, run to Bethel & do your worst;
when you get to Gilgal do some more;

bring your sacrifices every morning,
your tithes every three years:

& offer a sacrifice of thanksgiving with bread;
then proclaim & broadcast your offerings,

The Art of Prophecy

for that is just like you, children of Israel—
you think that will make it all better.

This is what YHWH says.

By Way of Apology

OK. Wow. Sorry about the preceding. Full-tilt prophecy can get ugly.

I got my major minor prophet knickers in a wad there. I should be past all that now . . . uh . . . I meant "am."

Am past that now.

But, here's the truth: "Amos" is nearly timeless in a major minor carbon prophet sort of way & the the "cows of Bashan" are so much dust (—but kind of fun here in post–carbonism) denigrated for all time among the carbon–ese. Remembered among the carbons only because they were offensive enough to make it into my little major minor prophet's rant.

Word.

In the dustheap of history, those rich folks who laughed at me . . . or didn't even see me standing there . . . are so much dust mixed in with all the other unknown dust. Dust puree!

Whoa.

Um. Sorry. That doesn't sound all that Properly Timeless and Over–It–All either.

I want to not care anymore. I want to forgive. Really I do.

The Art of Prophecy

Really. I want to give it all—by "all" I mean the fundamental unfairness of human history—give it all to the universe. Just pitch it like a penny into a nice dark fountain void & make a wish.

Yet even when you're very nearly timeless; even when you're a major minor prophet and dead and outside of time and carbon and all, some things are tough. (OK. Lots of things are tough. This ain't no travel brochure about the glories of being dead.)

I still can't see the Big Picture like . . . well, if You–Know–Who *is* a who . . . I mean, if You–Know–Who exists and sees and all that.

Thing is, the fine women who made up the Cows of Bashan contingent back in my carbon-based days, they're fine people now. Garden party set, you know. They have a fine time here outside of time. On the other side of carbon carbonating, ya know.

But they don't invite me to their garden parties. Sore winners.

Bless 'em.

Eclipse

There's one with a martini.
There's one with a lotto ticket.

There's one dying quietly with cancer.
There's one & another one.

There's all & all.
Living. Dying. Loud. Quiet.

For the earth swallows us all.
Tall. Diminutive. Posh. Poor.

Sheep of Takoa.
Cows of Bashan.

One big gulp &
all of us gone.

& then—back
something else is

again, carbon
carbonating.

What is it our poor curved backs can do?
We all of us hunch over the plow,
the keyboard, sewing machine. Bar.

The Art of Prophecy

One more round.
At 86,000 m.p.h.
What can we do?

We can do what we
can do for others.

We can do what we
can do for something

beyond our petty
carbon illusions.

That. That thing you can do is YHWH, if that sorta–proper little noun
works for you.
That thing that is a wild, joyous dance in the face of despair, dust & death.

In that way, I know the good 'ol boy exists!
Exists because he, she, it, or they don't have to.

There's no pressure, when you're top–dog god.

Here's an ethics exercise for you:

Is it about me? Bad.
Is it about institutions stamping on humanity? Bad.

> Does it increase the measure of love in the world? Good.
> Good! YHWH, by whatever name or definition or not at all, is there!

> "YHWH" is a good handle
> for pickin' up the pan.

Oh, my dears, dontcha know,
the silence is the biggest thing.
Biggest thing we have.
The nothing that is there.
The loudest voice out of the dark.
& out of the stars.

Eclipse

Silence. That is. That is the voice.

    I listened.
    I dusted off
    my broke–arse self

    & marched to the greatest city I knew.
    That's how it was for me.

    You choose. That's how the hell it will be for you.
    You choose. But that voice . . .
    That silence.
    That not–about–you–for–a–change . . .
    There 'tis. It's there. That's how it is.

    Sorry. But you . . .

    You, my dear, are just as responsible
    as me. Or Elijah. As Micah.
    Or Jesus, Buddha, MLK or Florence
    the–Hell Nightingale.

    As responsible to the people as Joan D'Arc or Maya Angelou.

    Whoever.
    You. You.

    You.

    Apologies for
    the intrusion.

    But . . .
    It's you.

Being Nearly Timeless
(† Being & Time, Take 2)

Think Frank Sinatra in a Shriner turban singing:

> Oh, I wanna be,
> I wanna be
> in the eighth century
> BCE.
> Yes, that's for me,
> that's for me,
> that eighth century
> BCE!

You don't hear that little ditty often, now do ya? Nope.

You might see yourself riding along with Napoleon. Or sitting in some salon with the *artistes* having tea & big ideas.

But Judah in the eighth century BCE. Not so much.

Here's what I know:. My crazy-arse time is every time. All times. Any time.

That's why I'm timeless. That and being dead.

We're all major in our minor little ways;
we're all minor in our major little ways.

Yet More Full-Tilt Prophecy

YHWH says:

You had clean teeth
because you chewed
no bread. Still, you
did not
listen to me.

> I stopped it from raining
> three months before the harvest,
> & I caused it to rain on one city
> & not on another.

One spot got rain,
Another spot dried up.
That is me!

> So it was that two or three cities
> wandered to one city for water,
> but they were turned away.
>
> Yet you have not listened to me,
>
> YHWH says.

I have smitten you
with blight & mildew.
When your gardens
& your vineyards

The Art of Prophecy

& your fig trees
& your olive trees
bloomed, the
locusts ate them,

   yet you have not listened to me,

   YHWH says.

I have sent pestilence,
just as I did in Egypt.

   I have killed your children
   with the sword,
   & I have taken away
   your horses.

I have made the stink of your camps
come right up your nostrils,

   yet you have not listened to me,

   YHWH says.

I have overthrown some of you,
as I overthrew Sodom & Gomorrah,
& you were like a firebrand
snatched out of the fire,

   yet you have not listened to me,

   YHWH says.

Amos's Famous Qualifications
for Being a Prophet:

1. Be an empty vessel.
2. Have no talents and few brains.
3. Be a misfit no one has ever understood.
4. Tell your truth even if it appears to be (even to yourself) nonsense.
5. Tell your truth loud and straight—as you see it, even if it looks daft, mad, or insane.
6. Prepare to die.

PART II

Penultimate Answers to Ultimate Questions

… & out
Of my misery I felt rising
A terrible anger & out
Of the anger, an absolute vow.

—Kenneth Rexroth ("The Bad Old Days")

what advice do the drowned have for the burned?
what gossip is there between the hanged & the buried?

—Danez Smith ("what was said at the bus stop")

When the Prophets and the Poets Call Out (Pharaoh's Estate Sale)

I.

Pharaoh's chariots doused
In a good dose of sea. Red.

This is the story
Of the possible
When it's called out
Long past despair.

It recurs,
This dousing,
& reoccurs.

Anytime *now*
Gets re-imagined.

Forget *The Times*.
Just read the times,
The possibilities with

The imagination loosed

From the wheels of
Pharaoh's spin doctors.

II.

The Art of Prophecy

Old Pharaoh's strength
Is a prosy power,
All in a row of
Un-imaginative
Un-imagination;

Pharaoh's power
Is a prosy strength
Of what must be
& can't
be

Otherwise.

III.

No, now never has
A champion or
A scribe much—

The instant
Goes begging

While pronouncements of the future,
Prognostications of the past

Congeal on & on,
Stone, stone, stone.

IV.

This *now*, so tenuous;
So fragile, this instant;
So gossamer it so seldom
Goes noted,
Gets called out,

How all may be
Re-imagined

When the Prophets and the Poets Call Out (Pharaoh's Estate Sale)

V.

Pharaoh hears the rush,
the whisper in the reeds,
That the future
Might be different,

Different from now
If the prose didn't

Keep falling into line

To dam the possibles.

Pharaoh knows
& hears water.

VI.

The future re-imagined if
Those poets, those prophets
Got loose on it now;

The story retold,
That the future
Is not inevitable;

Is not prose
All arranged
By the powers.

VII.

Pharaoh's chariots, doused
In a good dose of Sea . . . Red

When the poets see now
In its possibles;

The Art of Prophecy

When the prophets
Call out
What may be.

When the prophets
Call out
What might be,

Put out the sign:

Pharaoh's Estate Sale—
Emergency
Happening
Now.

Everything goes.

Some Things Don't Change

>Let justice
>roll down
>like waters
>& righteousness
>like a mighty stream.

Oh, yes. That sounds good shouted from any 'ol street corner, any 'ol time.

>War crimes. Ripping pregnant women open.
>Exiling whole populations. War crimes.
>
>No Geneva Convention in my day, you say?
>(You think you've got one in yours?)
>There is the law of basic human decency.
>There is the law of compassion.
>Always has been.
>Seldom gets heeded.
>
>Some things don't change.

Sure, nations have always convinced themselves of the righteousness of their own cause. Of their special destiny. & that their own righteousness & special destiny justifies whatever their powerful choose to do.

>Hogwash.
>Always has been hogwash.
>Always will be.
>
>>"Can a trumpet be blown in a city,"

The Art of Prophecy

I screamed in the streets,
 "& the people are not afraid?

Does disaster come to a city,
unless YHWH has done it?"

Ooops

Yes, that last bit is theologically problematic. Reflects the times I lived in, when the Devil wasn't getting his dues.

Or getting into his details.

> It's a tough call,
> what to say is up to
> "YHWH" &
> what can be chalked
> up to 'ol devil–y—poo.
>
> Or nature. But,
> you know how it is:
>
> rhetoric. It
> sounds good
> at the time.
>
> Those names worked.
> Others do in your now.

In my day, people didn't think one big YHWH did it all. They needed some rhetorical convincing. Nowadays? Well. Can you say "process theology"?

Yes, Life *is* a Beach,
But Have You Looked at Beaches?

> Humans. You think religion is about comfort.
> A way to be hopeful in the human condition.
>
> I gotta say, this puzzles me.

Who said—who told anybody—that human existence might be comfortable? Or hopeful? Or hap-hap-happy?

This puzzles me. In your universe that's flying apart, who said there's any rest? Except that is for hucksters and politicians.

> Look at a big, content, old mussel.
> He's got barnacles on his shell.
> He's at the bottom of a warm sea.
>
> & with every wave, he washes
> toward shallow water.
>
> With every wave
> he comes closer to
> the place a gull will find him,
> pick him up for a moment's
> exhilarating flight.
>
> Then bang! on a hard, wet beach.
> & drop him again.
> Until his old shell cracks just enough

Yes, Life is a Beach, But Have You Looked at Beaches?

for the gull's beak to dart into.
& dart. & dart. Until
all his precious flesh flies away
in the stomach of another.

It puzzles me,
why we try
so hard
not to see.

Who said religion offers comfort?

This puzzles me. Where I come from
truth aligns with reality.

& reality is . . . a beach,
you silly ol' mussel.

First Doxology (*Amos* 4:13–5:1)

Look:

The One who makes mountains
& creates the wind;

The One who puts the very
thoughts into our minds;

the One who makes
morning out of darkness,

& walks the high places
of the earth—YHWH,

L-RD of Hosts,
is that One's name!

Say Your *Doxa*

"Doxology." "Doxa," glory. "Logia." Saying.

My sayings about the glory of the universe.

OK. I don't mind admitting I'm bitter that I wore home-made clothes, not the latest purple, all my life. Everything was a little stretched, a little thin. A little not-right. Never top drawer.

Yet, I wrote my way out of nowhere.
My words. "Amos." It's my name.
And it's my book, baby.
A major one of the minor ones.

Yes, I'm bitter that I never got the chance to be top shelf. Top drawer. "A" list. That I'm all done and down in history as a major minor prophet. Not even considered a poet. OK. I'll chew some bitter fruit. Eat some crow.

I'm self-aware. (Now that I'm non-carbon-based.) I know I'm whining like Habakuk. & that everybody needs to be a personal-best sort of person. I get it. I got it. Thanks, Brother Sigmund F.

The question you've got to ask yourself, o, privileged one, is *why*?

How could it happen that the Southern Kingdom wasn't up to the snuff of the Northern? How could it happen that a shepherd wasn't up to the snuff of a banker?

How? Why? Who thought of that shite?

The Art of Prophecy

Why does a shopkeep mean less than a CEO?
Why do the farmers who feed us live in one world, the us who get fed in another?
Why are dead poets good, live poets bad?
Why does the priest get a salary with bennies while the prophet gets jailed or ignored or stoned? (And stabbed in the back, non–metaphorically?)

Why. & why.

Those sedate Buddha statues sell in high-end shops
while the real Buddhas, the living ones, wait for a bus
to get to the food shelf. Why? & why . . .

What to Look For

OK. I'll be fair. & balanced. We major minor prophets sometimes get our due.

In the *Talmud*—Makkot 24a to be exact—it says that all of the 613 laws of Judaism are contained in one of my lines: "Seek Me & live." (Not "me," Me. The Big Me. The Other. The not-your-own-ego. The all and every-darn-thing. You know, YHWH, as I called it in the day.)

OK, it doesn't sound as good out of context. But still. Not bad as a *Reader's Digest* of Hebrew thought: "Seek YHWH & live." Translated: Get outta yer own shite and do somethin'!

Not bad as a summary of most religious practice, the good sort anyhow: get over yourself 'n' do somethin'.

To do that, you don't even have to figure out *who* "YHWH" is or *if* "YHWH" is. Just get outta yer own way and outta your own dark place and get at it.

As a matter of fact, I'm pretty sure it's a waste of time, figurin' out the where, why, and if about the Good L-RD and Jehovah and YHWH and all. I've watched people working on that little question for nigh-on 3000 carbon years.

No results yet.

That Good L-RD thing is only what you manage to do with it.

The Art of Prophecy

Just sayin'. Words to the wise, & all . . .

Where Are Your Walls?

What is gathered now
will be scattered.

Walls stand a while
in the wind, then
fall. Again & again.

Eventually to rise,
then no more.

We build walls.
We build walls
against the wind.

& the walls fall
& the walls fall,

after the attack,
after the neglect.

Always, the tomorrow
when the walls
are gone is coming,

coming. And
more walls again.

Second Doxology (*Amos* 5:8–9)

You who turn justice to wormwood
 & throw righteousness away,

seek the One who made the Pleiades
& Orion, & turns deep darkness

into morning & darkens day into night,

who calls for the waters of the sea
& pours them on the earth,

YHWH is that One's name;
 the One who makes destruction
flash forth against the strong,

so that ruin falls upon
even the highest walls.

Talkin' YHWH

Only the heart sees clearly. And—duh—it don't see nothin'.

I know it's not likely I'm telling you anything new, but I also know it's hard, being a mature carbon-based being on the earth. Brother Paul. We don't see eye-to-eye very often, but he made the point nice-like:

> Nonetheless, we speak wisdom among them that are perfect: yet not the wisdom of this world, nor of the princes of this world, that come to nought: But we speak the wisdom of G–D in a mystery, even the hidden wisdom, which G–D ordained before the world unto our glory: Which none of the rulers of this world knew: for had they known it, they would not have crucified the Lord of glory. (*1 Corinthians* 2:6–8)

Yes, & that eternal sort of wisdom is spoken by the heart. Don't see; does a lot of talkin'. The heart, though, speaks a foreign language to most of us. We feel anger, but anger is just a child beating its bloodied fists against a wall; anger is merely hitting a horse that spooks & scares you. Anger is natural; but it's a wasted emotion. Won't get anything changed or done.

Anguish is the gut trying to get through to you; trying to speak your language; trying to tell you, help you, to change yourself, then change the world around you. Anguish says, "enough is enough." Anguish doesn't beat its fists against the wall. Anguish sees beyond the wall. Listen. You can hear it. You can even learn the language of that foreign land called the heart.

That's how to write

The Art of Prophecy

    & incite
    the revolution.

There's a big 'ol gulf fixed between tears & tearing. You can cry; I cry on a dime; but tearing something up or down—that requires some consideration.

Doxology. "Doxa" means "glory." Doxa is what happens when nature feels to you just too beautiful; just too awe–and–some to put into words. It's a gut thing; feeling thing; unspeakable thing. A foreign tongue. Then, when you feel that, you get your *doxa* on & you attempt in words what can't be said.

That's where *it* happens.

Here's the thing, campers: YHWH talks exactly as much today as YHWH ever did talk. Meaning *nada*. Not a thing.

It's a question of cleanin' out your ears, my dears. Call that "YHWH." Call it the universe, like my Brother Spinoza. Call it nothing. Just call it.

And that nothing you hear . . . That's all of it. Wow.

Brother Amos' (Nearly) Famous Formula for Prophecy & Poetry

1. Lose your mind.
2. Lose your self.
3. Listen to your heart.
4. Hear the silence.
5. Listen to your heart.
6. Say all you dare about this . . .
7. nothing.
8. This . . .
9. this . . .

    all there is.

The Primate Paradox

No one can be
Told anything*

That matters.

*Any word contains
other words in its
meaning & is
only part of
a system of words.

For every action
there is the choice;
there is the action;
then there is
the interpretation.

Every emotion has
a story, a history.

Human beings cannot act
outside of human nature—
all human actions
are human nature.

Third Doxology (*Amos* 9:5–6)

    The L-RD of Hosts
    is the One who touches
    the earth & it melts

    & all who live on it mourn,
    & all of it rises like the Nile,
    & sinks again,
    like the Nile in Egypt;

    that One builds rooms
    in the heavens & secures
    heaven's vault upon the earth;

    that One calls for
    the waters of the sea
    & pours them out on
    the surface of the earth—

    "YHWH" is that One's name.

(If you like.)

After the Doxa Comes the Work

Now hear this: the *doxa* all said, get this:
The universe is not a monarchy.
Except in this sense: everything is One.

A great big everything sort of One.

&, yes, that is on the final test.
Pass 'er fail, baby.
Ya gotta know it. In yer gut.
You're already one with all there is.
It's just that you've got to know it
& act that way. No "have to" about it.

Therefore, compassion is your spiritual practice;
justice is your spiritual practice.
Love is your *modus operandi*.
Say it with me, in a *noir* detective sort of voice,

"Love is my M.O." Oh, yeah. Fedora
and some ominous tones.

When you know with all our heart, soul, & being
that all that is deserves compassion & justice,
your only choice is to be a compassionate & just being,
& to act in love.

When you know with all your heart, soul, & being
that all that is

After the Doxa Comes the Work

is deeply & inextricably woven together,
your only choice is to work with
& for
compassion & justice.

Spiritual integrity is to act compassionately & justly.

But where to start, right?

Oh, that again. Damn . . .

A Suggestion

Here's a suggestion:
performance art.
Like my brother Isaiah:

> YHWH spoke to Isaiah
> son of Amoz, & said,
> "Go, & strip off your
> mourning clothes &
>
> take off your sandals."
> Isaiah did just that,
> & walked naked &
> barefoot three years
>
> as a warning to Egypt
> & Ethiopia—as he walked,
> so would young & old be
> led, naked & barefoot,
>
> butt–naked, to the shame of
> Ethiopia & Egypt. (20:2–4)

Way to frame it, Isaiah, buddy!

In all your prophet journey, think performance art!

The Work

is to find
& find the self

& find again
until you know

there's no
self there.

Love the other
other than the

self and live.

Wine in Bowls

It's curious, ain't it, that this wild, foaming cosmos has danced along always for we carbon creatures, yet we've put our faith in anything but.

That's surely what kept the Brothers Laotzi up at night. &

me. It's a mystery.

> Woe to those
> at ease in Zion,
> & those who trust
> Samaria's mountain,
> those called important
> in the nation, playing one
> country off against another!
>
> Go to Calneh & look;
> from there go to the great Hamah;
> & take a look,
> then go down to Gath of the Philistines.
>
> Are you somehow better than these kingdoms?
> Is your borders greater than their borders,
> you who keep thoughts of
> returning a favor far from your mind
> & trust in your own reign of violence?
>
> You who lie on ivory–studded beds
> & stretch out on couches,
> eating the lambs out of the flock
> & the calves out of the stall;

Wine in Bowls

you who chant to the sound of strings
& invent for yourselves
instruments of music to best David;
who drink wine out of bowls,
anointing yourselves with
the most expensive ointments

but take no notice of
the suffering of others.

For these things you will go captive
with the first that go captive

& the banquet of those who
helped themselves

will disappear.

Compassion Chant

From the flashing
visions, we are blind;
   from the luscious

music, deafened;
from the flowing
   words, dumb; now,

now we can see;
in this silence
   we can hear; we

can speak the still
& the small; we,
   after seeing,

hearing, speaking
silence, can be
   in compassion.

Can be
in love.

What Brother Ernst Bloch Said About Imagining

The possible is not
about what has been
up till now, but about

what has never been yet,
but could be, if
only we could see,

if only we might imagine,
the whole picture. Reality
is that which might be, if

only we imagine well enough
to keep ahead
of what happens next.

How to Blow It Out

Seek your source.
   Do your duty.
      Imagine what might be
in it for everything.

How's that sound as a plan?

Way I see it, these are the foundations of being;
formulators for thinking.
& touchstones against which we whet our daily action.

Unlike my Amorite & Nazarite references,
   seeking your source & doing your duty to
all that is stays constant
across time & culture, no?

That's how to incite,
how to write
the revolution.

That's how to keep your references current. Seeking the source of being implies a constant search, not an "oh, there it is!" approach. See? It implies that truth & reality are mysterious, moving targets. Going forward always. Why even name it, since that can be a stop?

This attitude is a gotta–do, I think, in order to keep each of us humble & to avoid the propensity toward judgment & violence that human flesh is heir to.

How to Blow It Out

It keeps us from hatin' on the Amorites.

Brother Louis Armstrong says,
  "If ya ain't got it in ya,
  ya can't blow it out."

Oh, Brother Louis is such a Zen master.

We've gotta search always every minute in order to get "it" in us.
We've gotta strive continuously to share what we have found.

  Don't name it.
  Do it.

Circles & Circles

Some of us have to stick our necks out.

Brother Rilke put it this way—

I live my life in circles that widen
and widen to reach out across the world.
I may not finish this final circle,
but I surrender myself to it.

    I circle around YHWH, around the ancient tower.
    I've been circling for thousands of years,
    & still I'm unsure: am I a falcon,
    a storm, or a great song?

The falcon circles;
    the falcon floats;
the falcon is there,
    yet never interacts,
    never commits.

    There are many falcons;
    we must have falcons;
    yet they little affect
    the world, in their circling.

We know the storm.
    We know the stormers.

They are most of us, content

Circles & Circles

   to do our own bidding,

like Brother Aesop's scorpion,
   stinging the frog carrying

the scorpion across
   the river,
   scorpions prepared
to follow our own whims,
   all the way to the bottom.

The storm is most of us.
Chief; Pharaoh; Caesar;
King; President;

Prime Minister. Pleb.
Storming & ceasing. &
   every moment believing
   we are giving, doing good.

Most of us are storms.
   Pharaohs of the home.
Pharaohs of the workplace.
   Pharaohs of corporations,

of banks. Pharaohs of the mind.
   Storms. Making the world less.
   Making the world what it is.

Some of us must
   stick our necks out.
Some of us must
   join into

the song of the universe,
   the chorus of free, loving community.

Some of us must see what is
   & call out what's wrong.

The Art of Prophecy

We must be a song, some of us.
   Singing for justice,
   compassion, love.

Picture This

I drew some pictures even Hollywood would like:

>I will load you down,
>like a cart
>
>under a load
>of sheaves.
>
>Then the swift will
>lose their running,
>
>& the strong
>their strength,
>
>& even the mighty
>will fail
>to save themselves.
>
>Archers will not stand;
>the swift of foot will not
>run fast enough;
>
>the fastest horse will
>not be swift enough.
>
>On that day, the bravest
>will run away naked.

Let's Play the Gnostic A-Go-Go

Yep, that's Creative Prophecy 101: create pictures that hurt.

Because we people, when we're not careful, let pictures run away with our minds. Then our minds create more pictures. And 'round and 'round she goes.

Take the Bloody Mary Game, for a for instance. Have you played that one?

> Go into a bathroom that has a mirror.
> Shut the door; turn off the light.
> Light a candle.

Spin around thirteen times, each time saying, "Hail! Bloody Mary!"

> Stop.
> Look in the mirror.
> What do you see?

Run out of the bathroom screaming.

Yep, Bloody Mary's in the mirror. Or, at least, *something* appears in the mirror. Goes to show what we human beings have always done in our own minds. With our own minds.

Fact is, we people can fool ourselves into seeing—imagin-in'—just about anything. Our imaginations can scare the daylights out of us; make us sick; make us well; make us saints. We can see Bloody Mary, even if we have no idea what Bloody Mary might really have looked like.

Let's Play the Gnostic A-Go-Go

(Actually, she's a fine person to have a pint with. But then, I wouldn't know a Protestant from a piss ant, ya know?)

Pictures. In our minds.

Have you ever considered that maybe YHWH remains an object of human desire because the human imagination just can't let go of something *that cool to imagine?* As my brother Isaiah said it,

> Yes, you are a G–D who keeps hidden,
> O, G–D of Israel, deliverer! (45:15)

Way to sum it up, bro. Yes, the best way to be famous is to be totally remote; totally unseen; totally Out There.

Image–N–Ary.

Special. You Want Special?

Special privileges mean more responsibility, no?

> Hear this word that YHWH
> speaks against you,
> O, children of Israel,
>
> against the whole family
> that I brought up
> from the land of Egypt:
>
> I have treated you best
> of all the world's families;
> therefore, I will punish you
>
> for all your wrongdoings.

That's just fair, don't you think?

Don't tell anyone, but I believe in karma:

You give.
 You get.
You know?

A Thought from the Ba'al Shem Tov

Where your
Thought is,

You are.

Who Gets the Word?

OK. I got off into the weeds on that last one.

Focus. Focus . . .

It all comes down to who yer workin' for—

> the Powers that Be or
> the Everything that Is.

As I said in my major minor book,

> Surely YHWH doesn't take
> a step without first tipping
> off the prophets.
>
> The lion has roared,
> who will not fear?
>
> YHWH has spoken,
> who can but prophesy?
>
> Preach in the strongholds of Ashdod;
> in the strongholds of Egypt,
> saying, Assemble yourselves
>
> upon the mountains of Samaria,
> & see the great tumults
> surrounding you,
> & the oppressed surrounding you.

Who Gets the Word?

YHWH says, They who store up
violence & theft in their strongholds
do not know
how to do right.

O, Say What You See!

Sometimes, I just have to dust off the old pipes and get out there and preach it. I sent this message to one of my homeless carbon sisters in San Francisco just last weekend:

> O, you who, even
> with the best telescopes,
> see almost nothing of
> this universe, call me
> old-fashioned if you like.
> I've been called worse—
> I can take it, & I can
> hand it back.
>
> The capitalist cattle are always mooing!
>
> When you take robbery & violence to the bank, what
> are you plannin' on drawing out, with interest, my friend? Huh?

Hey your cow-nesses, you say I'm an ignorant sheep-herd,?

> I'll call you a brackish cistern,
> a dank place where no streams
> flow to refresh your waters!

You've been called worse, you say? Maybe. Call me old-fashioned. It's true, as I have averred (good Luke-like term, "averred, no?) that I'm all about the desert & sheep dung. But my message is in the teeth of any capitol—Paris, Big Apple, wherever the Cattle of Bashan are in charge.

O, Say What You See!

Yeah, OK. I see less than four percent of the universe where I am too, but I know something about the Dark Matter lurking. & I'm tellin' my truth, right into the teeth of the power.

See that? Look with me, cows. Peer into that beating heart of the ninety-six percent darkness. Join me. Look deep. Hug it. Because it embraces you. Even you brackish cisterns.

That's how to deal with your heart–of–darkness palpitations. Pitty–patty–pitty–patty!

It's a little technique to get past all technique—look deep.

Now hear this! —the "true self" just ain't there. Nope. Just a little percentage in the dark. My bud the Buddha got that right.

What we see, perceive, as self is all false. Every iota.

(Get the Greek reference?)

The true, true self is the whole kit-n-caboodle of everything. The brackish cistern, the dank places, the streams, the waters!

> The star matter;
> the dark matter;
> the desert rock;
> the hidden waters;
> the cries of the predator.
> the cries of the killed;
>
> the true self is all that is;
> therefore, it's nothing at all.
>
> & mostly—at least
> ninety–six percent—
>
> dark matter.
>
> How 'bout that, rich cow babies?

The Art of Prophecy

When we act out of intellect & will,
we ain't gonna be doin' it for real.
We get tired. Cranky, even.

Intellect knows but
does not feel.

Will may act but
cannot sustain.

The pain's gotta be
moved from the brain,

(where it's all fancy words)

to the body, where it's felt,
where it's at; em–bod–ied.

Remember that anger/anguish thing I was talking about before?

No statistic about the number of starving people can get us out of our heads. Looking into the eyes of a starving person can. Get it?

Nothin' about the numbers of homeless is gonna move you. But take one look at my teeth!

When you feel injustice in your sinews & bones, then, then you can't stop workin' for justice. & you won't tire.

A prophet or a poet is a conduit, a mainline from the unknowable into a moment of clarity.

Light 'em up, friend!

Hear me, cows! There's a big 'ol butcher called Justice comin' your way!

And Justice ain't no vegan!

Dressin' Down the Egos

Oh, yeah. Oh, yeah. Bein' on your high horse is what bein' a prophet is all about.

I have to admit it's frustrating, preaching nowadays. People just keep movin' down the sidewalk, so you don't get more than ten, fifteen seconds. I feel for ya, being a prophet nowadays. The Cows of Bashan have tasers these days.

Back in my day, when everyone bought the idea of one g-d or another & most times five or six, it was easy to do a little preachin' with some good word-pictures & it was easier to stick a needle in people's egos. Now, all they see is a crazy person.

Heck, back then, most people believed in the Evil Eye. That'll make 'em listen a minute or ten. & that apocalyptic invasion thing always stopped 'em in their tracks:

> YHWH has sworn by YHWH's self;
> YHWH the L-RD of Hosts says,
>
> I despise the pride of Jacob
> & hate his strongholds:
> so, I will hand over the city
> with everything in it.
>
> & it will happen that,
> if there are ten in one house,
> they will die.

The Art of Prophecy

Then, when the mortician comes for bones,
he will ask those outside a house,
"Is anyone inside?"
& they will say, "No, g–d—damn . . ."

& the mortician will say,
"Hold your tongue! Do not
say the name of YHWH!"

Look: YHWH commands;
YHWH will smite
great house to pieces
& little houses to splinters.

Do horses run on solid stone?
Do we plow the sea with oxen?

You have turned justice into poison
& the fruit of righteousness into hemlock.
You who rejoice in things that are Nothing
say, "We have met the challenge by our own Strength."

But, look, I will raise up against you a nation,
O, house of Israel, YHWH says, the L–RD of Hosts;
& they will afflict you all the way
from the entering in of Hamath
to the river of the wilderness.

Everywhere.

Was the mortician thing too much? I think not. Give 'em word–pictures.
Give 'em stories. Play up that smiting trope.

Give 'em nightmares.

Do Mercy, Not Rights

Brother Hosea, another of us in the major-minor leagues, said YHWH wants mercy, not "sacrifices," doing mercy, not rote obedience. Way to go, bro.

Thing is, now I know my siblings from the other side of the world; now I know that we all see that compassion does the talking in our human religious understanding. Compassion says—this form of hurt that I see, it must not be.

Allow me the luxury of being clear: all things—be they laws, constitutions, economies, jobs-jobs-jobs, states, empires, my believed fatherland . . . what have you—they must have a human scale.

> Human scale. Must. Have.
> Non. Negotiable.

All human constructs must, first & foremost, take living things into account—reducing the suffering and increasing the flourishing of all living things.

> All. Constructs.

The greedy & the scared are always gonna hit ya with what they're going to be callin' "the practicalities"—"What would that mean for the nation?" "How can we pay for that?" "That's a slippery slope!" & such. Lies. Evasions. Trust me. I've looked into the serious faces of those in government; all buzy-ness. All so serious-ness. "It's just not practical!" "Someday, maybe; not right now."

The Art of Prophecy

Excuses!

Everything. Every "why" and "wherefore" takes a backseat to the moral obligation of doing the right thing for living beings. Brother Jesus said, "Don't worry about tomorrow, for tomorrow will bring its own worries. Today's trouble is enough for today." Or, the way those King James lads put it, "Sufficient unto the day is the evil thereof" (Matthew 6:34).

Excuses!

No. Really.

Practicality & time are excuses for doin' a whole lot a nothin', or worse. As in,

> "Sorry, have–not, you
> ain't gettin' squat."

You know the routine:

> "It'll take some time."

> "All in good time.
> Wait."

When time & practicality come up, out of the lips of the rich and powerful, you know you've got an excuse on your hands.

Excuses!

All to protect & to justify the sorry little greedy self.

Look at that artillery that points out from your walls—who do you think will get killed by that?

Often. Too often . . . usually, the artillery is killin' the people who point it.

As my brother the Buddha says,

"They're after me!"
"They're out to get me!"
"They want my things!"
"They want to destroy me!"

Think this way
& live in hatred.

"They're after me!"
"They're out to get me!"
"They want my things!"
"They want to destroy me!"

Stop thinkin' this way,
& you are free.

As I've said before, the starting point is that realization that your "you" is a text that's already been mostly written by your time & place & assumptions. Even your g–d is only a projection. As my Sufi brother Junayd put it, "The water takes its color from the cup containing it."

As you have surmised, I have lots of friends who like to talk these things over in the pubs. On the subject, Brother Jacques Derrida endlessly says through his pipe smoke, "there is no outside to the text."

Brother Osho says, "I am here to destroy your personality, to give birth to your individuality."

Admittedly, that sort of saying doesn't go well until you've had a few lifetimes, or a few pints, but you have to admit it's a worthy goal he's got. Your "personality" is the thing your social location builds for you—the walls you are taught to install artillery upon.

Your "individuality"? Well, thing is, in my neighborhood, what we learn is that there ain't no individuality. No self. You break down those laughable walls built by society, you tear down the barricades and throw the artillery into the sea, and you find a fragile, frightened little primate: You.

Then . . . Then, you're gettin' somewhere. Or at least you're ready to be gettin'.

But then, no—let's just face it—you ain't really listening, are you?

Are you?

Formula One

New
Poem,

New
Mind.

Picture This

OK. Yes, statistics can sometimes be made concrete. I think this one works:

> Hear these words that I speak against you,
> even a lamentation, house of Israel.
>
> The virgin of Israel is fallen;
> she will rise no more;
> she is forsaken upon her land;
> there is none to raise her up.
>
> YHWH says this:
>
> The city that marched out a thousand
> shall come back a hundred;
> the city that marched out a hundred
> shall come back ten to the house of Israel.

How's that for saying "ten percent"? Huh?

Consequences Have Elections

Silkworms weave
Their threads

For protection.

We kill them for
Their thread.

Lonely Plane

If you're thinking of going somewhere, try your own mind.

>This is what YHWH says:

Seek me & live.

>Don't seek Bethel,
>don't go to Gilgal;
>do not pilgrimage
>to Beer-sheba, for

Gilgal will go into captivity,
& Bethel will come to nothing.

Seek the L-RD & you will live;
otherwise, YHWH will break out
like a fire in the house of Joseph,

devouring you,

& there will be none
to quench it in Bethel.

Can You Say "Flexible"? How 'Bout "Tenable"

How's that for saying there's nowhere to run? Poor primates. We've always been so into running somewhere safe & calling it sacred or holy.

Now hear this: everywhere is holy. All places. Every little square centimeter of this cosmos is perfect & holy. Putting your G–D on an alter or a shelf somewhere, some place, is a fool's game. & it leads to street fights. Holy is sacred and visa versa, even if it's dangerous.

Let's just ask ourselves an obvious question: Why can't we admit that "YHWH" is a flexible concept? An evolving one. & often a battlefield rather than a reason for reconciliation. & lots of that fighting stuff is over where & what & when some g–d or other wanted something or other; said something or other.

Makes ya wanna chuck the whole human thing into the ash bin, don't it?

Yet, how will human beings ever be just or righteous without a vision of justice & righteousness? & you think governments are going to give us that? Uh. No. They're all about practicalities. Governments are in the hooves of the Cattle of Bashan.

OK—the vision that creates justice doesn't have to be "YHWH." But YHWH is a good place to start for lots of people, because they were born into that manner of speaking. To the manner born. So, how do we start there?

    How do we find a commons

The Art of Prophecy

for creativity, wisdom, meditation,
truth, ecology, values, justice,

activism . . . com–passion.

You know what get's you called a prophet?
When you call people to love one another.

There's nothing more subversive than that.
Love is always countercultural.

Quote me. Sound bite me on that.

Prophets break down borders;
love breaks down borders.

A prophet—in case you're hoping to become one of us—asks simple questions. Because those ones, they are the damn difficult questions.

The tough questions . . . the ones that must be asked, sound childish.

Prophets are all about passionate provocation.

Ask yourself a simple question of the next thing you do:

    What if everybody did that?

Brother E. Kant, Prophet, thought that one up, & it's a good question.

Here's another one:

Why is there some good in the world?

Go ahead, get your chin in your palm & do a brown study on that one. Why would there be any good among human beings? They're a buncha darn carbon–based primates.

Love is always countercultural. Try it.

Can You Say "Flexible"? How 'Bout "Tenable"

Focus. As Brother Jesus said, "The light of the body is the eye; therefore, if you focus on the light, your whole body will fill with light" (Mathew 6:22 KJV).

I'll admit, that particular Jesus is sounding a bit New Age there. He gets an A for image, though.

& I know, I know—I'm supposed to ask "why is there something rather nothing?" I don't find that question particularly interesting. If there were nothing, I wouldn't have to ask questions. There wouldn't be any boots on any heads. Wouldn't be anybody prostituted in any temples.

You're asking questions, ergo, there's something rather than nothin'.

Duh.

Seriously, the question is why human beings do any good at all. Think of that old cliché—cutting off your nose to spite your face. Fact is, we human beings are capable of unenlightened self-destruction & I mean most of the time. We're half-way done cutting our noses off our face before we even think about it.

Between self-destruction & self-distraction, we live our lives.

Write that down.

So what does it mean to exit that circle?

We start asking what others need. We seek the well-being of others.

Why? Could it be when we, all the way back in human time, realize that there are no others? That we are all one?

No, you don't need the varied and various G–D concepts to get there, but lots of people have lived in that place. And it has done at least a smidgen of good. If it works, use it. If not, not!

Don't try to dodge this: I know because I was alive once, carbon-based once: Humans go around thinking things have some sort of essence that matches our reaction to things. Our subjective reaction. We resonate, as the cliché goes:

> "Red means something because it makes me think of anger."

> "That stinks. It makes me sick to my stomach."

> "Those people are not like us."

Hogwash! It's all the same. Still, that resonance is the beginning of action. And the beginning of wisdom. And compassion.

Go ahead, try it: resonate, why don'tcha?

Where I'm At

Don't get me wrong. We're all headed to the same place, more or less. There's no distinction here in near-eternity between the good & the bad. The cows & the pharaohs & dictators & tax collectors & bankers all end up just fine.

I have a few pints with my sort, and visa-versa.

Sometimes, I suppose, I *wish* there were such a thing as the hell the Christians thought up. That the rich really got their due. Yet YHWH—or the universe or whatever—knows we've got this little human trait called self-delusion.

That "arc of the universe" and all that . . . delusion.

Let me clue you in on the hereafter. Everybody achieves compassion. I got compassion—even for the Cows of Bashan. Yep, even they have that Nirvana thing goin' on; Brother Buddha got it—some got at it in the illusion called life.

But death. Well, all I can say is, try it. & . . . oh, you will!

& after you drink that Kool-Aid, baby, you ain't pointin' no fingers! You are all love after that. Can't help it. Death is your PhD in compassion. When you're free of that carbon base, you're flyin' high, baby. Oh, yeah.

> Signed, sealed, delivered.
> So. It's just a matter of time, ya'll.

The Art of Prophecy

> No, saints like me don't have all the fun.
> We cut you in. Just takes a little
> rearrangement of priorities is all.
>
> If you wanna be a saint, I mean.
> When you're carbon-based I mean.
>
> Here's how to do it: *be obsessed.*
> Be completely, utterly *obsessed*,
> every moment, obsessed with liberation—
> liberating everything from suffering.

That's it. Brother Buddha nails it. That's all you have to do. Wake up . . . thinking it. Go to bed thinking it. Eat, sleep, urinate & defecate the liberation of all beings from suffering.

It is what Brother Shantideva calls "exchange of self & other."

> See yourself as you once saw others:
> not much; not at all.
> See others as you once saw yourself:
> everything. Ultimate importance.

Self-protection. Looking for happiness. Getting what you want. I'm just sayin', though I've already said there's no hell—the road to hell is paved with self-regard.

Brother Shantideva said it up straight: "Whatever suffering there is in the world flows from the wish for your own happiness. Whatever happiness there is in the world flows from the wish for the happiness of others."

> You there, primate, with your finger against your chin.
>
> Thinker. Watcher of flames. Drinker of hops and grapes. You know that you still can't agree about whether the mind is a function of the brain.

Just sayin'.

I See You!

Taking & giving. Paint a picture:

    Look, the eyes of YHWH see the wrongs in this kingdom.
    This is what YHWH says:

    I will wipe your kingdom off the face of the earth,
    except that I will not utterly destroy the house of Jacob.

    I will command, & I will sift the house of Israel
    among all nations, just as meal is sifted in a sieve,
    yet not a single grain shall fall upon the ground.

    All the wrongdoers among my people—
    those who say "evil will not catch up to us or stop us"—
    shall die by the sword.

    On that day I will raise up the fallen tabernacle of David & patch the holes.
    I will raise up the ruins & rebuild it, so that it will be as it was in the old days.

    They will possess a remnant of Edom
    & all the foreign lands where my name is honored.

    Look, the days are coming, YHWH says,
    when the plowman shall overtake the reaper,

    & the treader of grapes the sower;
    & the mountains will drop sweet wine,
    & all the hills will melt.

The Art of Prophecy

    & I will bring my people of Israel out of captivity,
    & they will rebuild the wasted cities & inhabit them;

    & they will plant vineyards,
    & drink the wine from them;

    they shall also make gardens,
    & eat the fruit from them.

    I shall plant them upon their land,
    & they shall be pulled up no more
    out of their land
    which I have given them,

    YHWH says so.

Again, admittedly, not mine. Added to my little book named Amos. But inspired by little 'ol major minor you-know-who.

Way to paint a picture, nameless scribe!

I should try to look that guy up!

Prophet's Sound

Single thread
　of a spider's weaving
Flashing in the sun.
　It is the noise

That births silence;
　it is the dark
Sets off the light.
　It is the words;
It is

The not that
　Bears is, be
　　Without was.

Now without never.
　It is the breath

Drawn deeply.
　Let go.

　Let
　go.

All the Wealth

Think of all that money,
　all that money when
　all the people are gone . . .

Think of all that wealth
　all those riches when
　all the humans are dead.

Think how rich
　the rodents will be
　once all the people

have gone.

Talk about

Kah–ching!

Pick Your Disaster; Pick Your Why

Here's what I've spent about three thousand years wondering: is there a difference
between perception & imagination?

I'm not talking about coming up with more precise definitions for these terms. I want to know how these two ideas work in our minds & hearts.

I mean, do these two just go around & around, the engine generating our reality? Perception, imagination; imagination, perception. Repeat. *Ad infinitum* . . .

Take this one of my little rants, as example:

> YHWH has shown me this:
>
> Look, YHWH formed grasshoppers
> at the second sprouting,
> after the king's mowings.
>
> & it came to pass that
> when they had made an end
> of eating the grass of the land,
> then I said, O, L-RD YHWH, forgive,
> I beg you. Who will help Jacob
> Rise? He is so small!
>
> YHWH was sorry for doing this.
> It will not be, YHWH said.
>
> YHWH has shown me this:

The Art of Prophecy

Look, YHWH called for a rain of fire,
& it devoured the sea,
ate up a part of it.

Then I said, O, L-RD YHWH, stop,
I beg you. Who will help Jacob
rise? He is so small!

YHWH was sorry for doing this.
This will not be either, YHWH said.

YHWH has shown me this:

Look, YHWH stood upon a wall
that had been built with a plumb line.
YHWH had a plumb line in hand.

YHWH said to me,
Amos, do you see this?

I said, Yes, it's a plumb line.

Then YHWH said,

Look, I will set a plumb line
in the middle of my people Israel.
I will not let them get by with all this again.

The high places of Isaac will be desolate,
& the sanctuaries of Israel will be laid waste;
& I will rise against
the house of Jeroboam with the sword.

See my question? What is perception, what imagination? It's really crossin' a line, saying I saw YHWH on top of a wall. Yet, see how you don't want to call me on it?

"Heck, yer just makin' shite up anyway," you say?

Imagination?

Pick Your Disaster; Pick Your Why

or perception?

You see, even if maybe, perhaps, it didn't quite happen like I describe it here, all this happened, the disaster part.

Was what happened in history really YHWH's punishment? Or just the chaos of empires butting their heads & kicking the asses of the little people?

Or do you want to vote for a little of both?

Perception
or imagination?

Can't quite see YHWH up there on the wall? How about that plumb line?

How about the idea that there's a direction & purpose to human history?

Perception. Imagination. & on. & on . . .

The End Is . . . Apocalyptic

The End! The End! The End! Some people always want the end.

    For lots of reasons people want The End.
    Some want wrongs righted.
    Some want the boredom to stop.
    Some wish their own time to be in some way unique.
    Some fear the other way the world may end: their own death.

    The Day of YHWH gets quite a bit of press,
    fulfilling as it does so much wishful thinking.
    Like asking someone her favorite Beatle,
    asking someone what he thinks
    The Day of YHWH might accomplish
    reveals a great deal about a person's personality
    & world view.

    Here's what my human self had to say about the coming Day of YHWH:

      Too bad for you who desire the Day of YHWH!
      Why would you want the Day of YHWH?

      It is a day of darkness, not light,
      as if someone fled from a lion
      & met up with a bear;

      as if someone went into a house,
      resting a hand against the wall,
      & was bitten by a snake.

The End Is . . . Apocalyptic

The Day of YHWH is darkness, not light,
& gloom with no glimmer in it. (5:18–20)

(Repeating) Amos's Famous Qualifications for Being a Prophet:

1. Be an empty vessel.
2. Have no talents and few brains.
3. Be a misfit no one has ever understood.
4. Tell your truth even if it appears to be (even to yourself) nonsense.
5. Tell your truth loud and straight—as you see it, even if it looks daft, mad, or insane.
6. Prepare to die.

PART III

What is Struggling to Be Born?

…dismiss whatever insults your own soul, & your very flesh shall be a great poem & have the richest fluency not only in its words but in the silent lines…

—Walt Whitman

And suddenly we see
that love costs all we are
and will ever be.
Yet it is only love
which sets us free.

—Maya Angelou

Words in the heart are not words.

—*The Talmud*

Let Me Explain How It Works

Yes, the general tenor of science leads one to assume that the mind is a function of the brain. As I say, all you have to do to prove this is get drunk.

Voila. Brain in the mind, mind in the brain. Then you throw up.

But wait. Take a vinyl record. Smash it. Is the music still there? Sure, if you can glue that record back together. Or if you're willing to pony up some more bucks to buy another one.

But wait. Take that record player. Smash it. Is the music still there? Sure, you're out more money, but you can put the music on a new device & . . . Voila. There's the music.

So, what is the mind, the consciousness?

Is it the record? The file? The player? Or the music . . .

> There's Sister Ella Fitzgerald. Wait. Can't be. She's dead.
> There's Brother Eric Satie . . . no. Even deader.
> But they are there.
> They are here.

> So. *You* work it out, smart person.
> Work it where you are at.
> Or just wait. I'll meet you when
> you're at where I'm at.

The Big An-swers

1.

Here's a big question: What is?
Here's a big answer: Human beings don't know.

The empires.
The nations.
The kings.
Nobody.
Nobody knows.

You can stand on your head
& spit nickels;
It don't matter—

'Round 'n' 'round it'll go.

Nobody . . .
Nobody knows.

2.

Yet you don't, you see
Need to put
Anything together—

It's all together,
That anything . . .

The Big An–swers

It's presumptuous to put
Anything together.

3.

Dark those branches
Reaching down,

Veins into flesh.
Duration;
Interval;

Time . . .

4.

When a symbol
Is what it is . . .

But . . . no,
Couldn't be.

But if it were
What it is,

A symbol . . .

5.

Priests & kings.
Kings & priests live in fear.
Like nerds
At a party,
Priests & kings are afraid.

They don't want to say.
They don't want to say.
They don't want to say

The Art of Prophecy

What they know,
Those kings & priests

At the party.
Clarity. Oh, clarity
Is what they fear.
Those priests & kings,
Clarity at their
Own party.

6.

We're all
Checking out;
All checking out,
We
Priests & kings
At the party.

Clarity is us,
We are clear, we
Kings & priests
At the party.

I will be grace, &
you will be clarity.

How will that be?

7.

Oh, sure let's
Just say, shall we,
There's a G–D
Shaking a spear,
Shaking a spear;

Sure there's a G–D

The Big An-swers

& priests & kings,

Shaking. Let's
just say.

Shallow as a Puddle; *De Profundis*

How will your life be—puddle or profound?

Think "concinnity:" total, harmonious, whole,
all put together quite nicely, thanks.
That's what it is. It's easy to see that,

looking out at the stars. It's easy to see
that, looking at ants at work. Or even
looking at war. It's easy to see in the flow

of blood or milk. Not so easy to see in
movements of we, us. Manunkind,
as brother cummings calls us. Not easy.

Yet the flow of our history, in its murder
& hope, moves like the stars, like the
rivers, like blood when your own edges

have gone at last away. That too, too
solid flesh Bro Shakespeare talks about.
When your own edges have gone, then

the flow of humanity on & on
too can be seen

at last. That. That's prophecy, baby!

Where We're Comin' From (& Free Will Too)

Go ahead, tell the earth to stop spinning.
Resist the seasons. Insist
That there be no day & night.
No aging. No time. Go ahead.

Knock yourself out. Deny
All fourteen billion years
Of the universe flying apart.
Resist truth as it trundles along.

Call me a skeptic.
I'm old enough to take it.
We live a little while,
Learning what we can.

Knowledge. That goes on after we're dust.

Limits. Limitation. Oh, we hunting animals.
How might we manage to see what
Won't feed us? Microwaves.
Sonic waves. Gimme a break.

Yet, we can hunt
what we can't see!

The way we got here—
The paths & roads—
That's how we think.

The Art of Prophecy

Hard to think otherwise.

Every way, because each
Is predetermined,
Is misguided. Wrong
Direction.

We are what we are born,
But then there's the frosting.
The names of things
We learn to smear on
Too thick.

What we think stinks;
What we desire. Then
There's a more here
& standard there, beaten
In or hugged close, in
whatever time we're born.

We're birthed on a path.
But after that
The steps we choose
Might be our own; or
May be the choices we're

Taught.

The choice is yours, but
How do you choose
To choose it?

Yes, Brother Albert has it—
It's all relative. Except
When it's our own asses.

Who told you
Death's bad?

Where We're Comin' From (& Free Will Too)

I'm just sayin'.

Death. Beauty.
Stench or savor.

I'm just sayin'.
This free will
Thing.

It's all about

Where you're
Comin' from.

Being Nearly Timeless
(& Being & Time, Take 3)

Here's the question, if you've got the guts to ask yourself:

> Is religion the gift
> of the great beyond,
> a far out there
> something?

> Or is religion the gift
> of the human mind,
> a something
> in our brains?

"Work, for the night is coming," Brother Luther loves to shout. & so it is so many dour and serious folks make religion so much work for themselves and everybody else.

What are you afraid of? Are you worried there really is a G-D, & that G-D is so far beyond your comprehension that it appears—He, She, It, or They—is just jokin' around?

Do you fear that the sheer art of it all makes it so much play?

Ask an artist who has drunk herself to death how much play there is in art.

Ask any artist, even the living ones. The joy & the pain. Who can reconcile those? There is no balance in any angel's hands that will say a truth there.

Being Nearly Timeless (& Being & Time, Take 3)

A roll of the dice. As Brother Mallarmé put it. Is no game for the Awakened Ones.

Oh, no.

A ride on the train. On the wheel. On life itself. The artist. The artist throws all the chips on every spin.

Bet against us!

Bram Stoker is here, in this other-side-of-something. & what about that surly landlord who collected his rent?

Gone. In the sands of time.

No, there's no hell. But only the shiny ones glitter here in this nearly-eternal dark.
This is the insight. The truth. The obelisks of government officials, of Ptolemys & Others. So much dust. So much space under a car park. They gave only darkness in their lives; & the cosmos returns the favor.

& a painting? A poem?

Results, baby. Just look at the long-term results. Because art, now—that's YHWH's business.

I'm just sayin'.

Think about it: Why did the Big Gal (or Guy or They) ever create *anything*? Boredom? Ennui? Angst?

Some Big Plan?

A book of poems? A symphony?

Hey, you know, let's not be gossips about who is sleeping with whom. What do we *know*?

The Art of Prophecy

I think I know that
it's all a great huge dance.
I think I see that.

A dance. So, you see how quickly
it becomes about art?

Dance!

(Seriously. Stick with me here.)

Are we going to cede religion to the boring & the dull? The dour and seriously dusty? To those who know only how to put the right foot forward?

To those who don't believe in something as seriously fun and artistic as the Theory of Evolution?

Gimme a break!

Brother Darwin is a dancing sort of guy.

Brother Falwell? Gimme a break!

Take a little trip with me. See if religion is art. Is play.

& the danger? Your sanity. Only your sanity. Which ain't much, just sayin'.

If you define that to be _____ . . . name yer blank!

Music has so long been . . . of the spheres! Way up there. Beyond. See how them spheres do sphere!

Visual art. Not so much. Only because. It was so hard to . . . separate it from buildings.

& poetry. Well. Isn't that just words. Used another way or not? Or. Otherwise. What is it?

Can we humans give form to the formless?

Being Nearly Timeless (& Being & Time, Take 3)

The answer is *yes*, in spades!

Look at Las Vegas.

What could be a more concrete answer to meaninglessness?

Is life meaningless? Ka–ching. Ka–ching!

Not that Las Vegas is in any way unique. Look at Babylon. Look at Samaria. Look at Los Angeles.

Look at what you did yesterday afternoon.

Follow the money, baby. That way lies Antichrist.

& what–have–you.

It is the answers that kill us.
Can that come through?

The answers are the evil.

The echo of ego.

Kick that plasticine bag to the side because you have realized this: there are more answers than there are questions. The answers are safe. Comfortable. Ersatz.

& lies.

Art. Art Art.

Imagine. Ation.

Roll 'Em 'n' Swim for It

An unexamined life ain't worth livin'.
   Brother Socrates says so.
But 'ol Soc falls down on
   how to do the examining.

Seems to this ghost you've
   gotta make the trip
   from delusion to insight.
From hypocrisy to sincerity.

From "I—me—mine" to "we—be—us."

It's a life that takes the trip
   from delusion to profusion.
From self-deception to *per*ception.

From me to we; from fogging
   everything up
   to a sunny day;
from shallow lies to deep truth.

The unexamined life is not only
   not worth living—it's
not lived at all anyway.

It's got through. You can't
swim in a puddle, after all.

Speaking of Soc and his Pal Plato
This is the Western Story

We are chained
in a cave;
each of us
always have been,
staring, staring at
the cave wall.

The cave is all we
have ever known.

Images appear there,
shadows thrown
by a large fire
behind us.

Shadows. This is
all we know.
All we have ever
known. We are
watching shadows.

These shadows cast
are the shapes of things—

table. Horse. Human.

The Art of Prophecy

Some. Some of us
rebel. Wrench free. &,
climbing to surface,

see the things themselves
in their hazy truth,
blinded as we are
by the sudden light.

Shadows. Real things.
Here below.
Heaven.
Our minds.
The mind of YHWH.
This is the Western story
By Soc's pal Plato.

We draw a line between
olam hazeh,
this world, &
olam haba,
the world to come—

olam haba named
the good one, the one
not here, the outside,
rather than what we
have, the everyday—

whether this other place,
this *olam haba*, is heaven
above or heaven on earth,

the outcome is the same—
thinking the here &
the now aren't real enough,
not for us, oh no.

This is the Western story.

It's rubbish.

Rebels to the Surface!

Plato's Cave, oh, boy—
it gets at the idea we've
always had, fueled
the aspirations
of metaphysical rebels
like me. Those who strive
to be free of illusion.

Olam hazeh,
this world, &
olam haba,
the world to come—
the present
& the possible.
Basic Western thinking.

It is a basic error
—a real screw up—
in how we see. Has to be
gotten past by those
who strive to hear
the voice beyond. The truth.
That cave thing is bollocks.
The true illusion.

There is no cave.
There are no shadows.
There is no dualism.

Rebels to the Surface!

No two things.
No ideal.

There is only the haziness
of trying to see in the brilliant sun.

There is only the real.
Here. Now. Directly
to be seen.

Invisible;
silent;

the spaces between;
the space that is space;

the nothing that is nothing.

Myth & Cave

But Bro Plato just happened
to sum it up. It's long
been the fly in
the Western world's

ointment. The way
the story has gone,
& for a long time

I listened & thought
of ways to escape
the cave into light

& thought myself
a rebel of light.

Then one day
I opened my eyes
& I saw—

There's no cave
& no light,
only The One

where we all
are always
& everywhere—

always the light
is there—we only
need open our eyes.

Olam hazeh,
this world, &
olam haba,
the world to come—
they are One.

No walls; no fire;
no shadows;
no invisible friends;
no deceivers—

except ourselves.

The Climactic Confrontation (Part I)

Location: Bethel. Beth–El, the House of El.

Beth–El. The place Jacob used a stone for a pillow & had his dream of a ladder. Jacob set the pillow–stone up, a stele, anointing it with olive oil.

That place. That stone stayed. Began to be seen as sacred—the very one Jacob set up & anointed. Bethel. The place El dwells.

Vatican of the Northern Kingdom. The Cows weren't about to hear me in Samaria, so I headed to Bethel for some more abuse.

Amaziah, the head priest of Bethel, sent a message to King Jeroboam II:

"Amos is conspiring against you right in the very heart of your power. The so–called prophet Amos is saying that Jeroboam will die by the sword & that Israel will most certainly be led away from the land into captivity. The people can't bear to hear his lies. What shall I do with this YHWH-less traitor?"

The word back for 'ol Jerry the Second? "Let the fool talk. No one listens to those sorts of fools."

> Amaziah said to Amos,
> "O, you seer—go.
> Run back to Judah.
> Eat bread & prophesy there.
> Prophesy no more at Bethel,
> which is the king's chapel
> & the king's court."

The Climactic Confrontation (Part I)

"Seer"! "Seer" he called me. "Fake." "Charlatan." A professional for hire!

So, I talked back:

> I am no prophet,
> nor am I a prophet's son.
> I am a shepherd &
> a gatherer of figs.
>
> But as I followed the flock,
> YHWH took me & said,
> 'Go, prophesy to Israel.'
>
> So, hear the word of YHWH.
>
> You say, 'Prophesy no more at Bethel.
> Speak no more against the house of Isaac.'
> But just hear what YHWH says:
>
> Your wife will become a prostitute in the city,
> & your sons & your daughters will fall by the sword,
>
> & your property will be divided;
> & you will die in a foreign land.
>
> Israel will surely go into captivity."

Mic drop!

Being Nearly Timeless
(& Being & Time, Take 4)

Now that I'm outside of carbon and time, I've learned the hard way that every moment of existence in time contains the lesson we need at the time. Got that?

When time stops, there's no more good time for anything.

That's a problem. Because the moment's lesson isn't always clearly relevant. Why did my sandal strap break? Why did my horse throw a shoe? Why is the tire flat? How is this priest going to go about making me dead?

Lessons in the moment. Teachings we need for that moment.

Nope, not always clear. Seers, charlatans, professional priests—they don't have to live in the moment; they don't have to listen to the universe. They've got their marching orders from the Powers That Be.

But us. Us prophets. We've got to be in the moment, writin' away. Like the old song goes, "you gotta get up every mornin' an' plow." If you're going to write the revolution of the heart.

> Just got to trust the universe
> & let the lessons seep in.
>
> When it's gotta be
> just what I–me–mine wants,
> that's when The Real
> is gonna kick my ass.

Being Nearly Timeless (& Being & Time, Take 4)

When I'm doing what
practicality tells me,
that's when I'm only
a puppet of chance.

That's how the big
'ol wheels of the mills
of the earthly g-ds grind.

It's when we're trying
what can't be done
that we look weak.
Powerless. But we're

full of potential. When
we let go of ego
& tie our wagons
to "can't be done."
That's when; that's
when possibility

breaks in. Boom.

It's Not About Under-standing or Standing Under. Nope

It's not about understanding. Can I say that any plainer?

> & it ain't about worshiping
> in the right pose
> or the cor-rect clothes
>
> or the proper di-rection
> or according to con-vention.

I said it pretty good,
if I do say so myself:

> Hate evil;
> love good;
> work some
> justice
> at the gate.
>
> Hate evil;
> love good;
> work some
> justice in
> the world.

First rage, then action.

That's the kind of "seeking" I'm talkin' about! Seeking is about doing somethin'—gettin' somewhere for somebody. That's the way I was

It's Not About Under-standing or Standing Under. Nope

thinking when I came up with those lines that Brother MLK liked so much:

I hate—I despise—
your festivals;
I take no delight in
your uptight assemblies.

Though you offer me
burnt offerings
or grain offerings,
I will not accept them.

No, I will not heed
the fattened beasts
of your peace offerings.

Spare me the noise
of your songs!
I will not listen to
the melody of your strings.

Instead of all that falderal,
let justice roll down like water,
& righteousness like a mighty stream.

That's in my book, chapter five, verses 21 to 24. Yep. Look it up. I said that. This here major minor prophet said that.

"Justice" & "righteousness."

"Righteousness"—living right. "*Tzedek*" to be exact. Ethical action.

Ohhhh, yeah. Oh, yeah. I was cookin' that day. Go, me.

Religious people! We're the best & the worst of humanity all rolled into one enchilada.

Holy day this, holiday that.
Burn this, toast that. Put
your fancy togs on. Get

    yourself a big 'ol hat &
    call yourself important.
    Religious people! Like that.

Or . . . do some good for this poor earth & its suffering living things.

It's a choice, people! Duh!

Givin' Me the Willies

Don't get me wrong. Religion is good for all kinds of things. Or, rather, "good" is not maybe the best word. Religion is "effective" in producing all kinds of results.

But let's face it: Making a human being act in a moral, ethical manner is *not* one of the things that religion does well.

Much more likely as an outcome of the practice of religion is socially-enforced & reenforced behavior. Behavior that benefits somebody, be that body the self—unlikely (unless you already be at the top)!—or the ruling elite—very likely!

Brother Shakespeare always gives these guys a break. How many times do I have to hear "uneasy lies the head that wears a crown"? I may never offer *him* an ale again. Thing is, Brother Willy really seems to believe that Princess & the Pea malarky about rulers being all about ruling well & self-sacrifice & goin' around bein' all special.

My achin' back, Bill!

Get a clue!

The Value of Thought & Belief

Of what use is a teaching or a practice that does not lead to any change in the world?

Of what use is a spiritual experience that does not lead to change in behavior?

If you are convinced that you are a frog, but you don't try to jump, what is your conviction?

If you are convinced that compassion & justice are the purpose of life, yet you do not live for compassion & justice, what has changed?

Here's another moral truth: you can believe in the best of actions yet still act in a morally reprehensible manner.

Only those thoughts that trigger action have validity. Thought & belief have no meaning outside of action. As Brother Frantz Fanon said it, "What matters is not to know the world but to change it."

Amen on that!

The Climactic Confrontation (Part II)

The crowd crowded in while I proclaimed there, outside the temple:

> YHWH has shown me this:
> a basket of summer fruit.
>
> YHWH said, Amos, what do you see?
> I said, A basket of summer fruit.
>
> YHWH said to me,
> The basket has come to
> gather my people of Israel;
>
> They will not get away again.
> The songs of the temple
> will be howlings on that day.
>
> YHWH says this: There will be
> dead bodies everywhere.
> You will cast them
> into the street in silence.
>
> Hear this:
> you who swallow up the needy,
> bringing ruin to the poor of the land,
> saying, When will the new moon be gone,
> So that we may sell grain?
>
> When will the Sabbath be gone,
> so that we may offer wheat,
> making the weight small & the shekel great,
> & falsifying the weights by deceit?

The Art of Prophecy

Deceit, so that we may buy the poor with silver
& the needy for a pair of sandals.
Yes, & selling the husks of the wheat?

YHWH has sworn by the pride of Jacob,
Surely I will never forget what you have done.

Shall not the land tremble for this, &
everyone mourn who dwells there?

It will rise up like a flood,
Like the waters in Egypt,
& you will be cast out & drown.

On that day it will come to pass,
YHWH says, that I will cause
the sun to go down at noon,

& I will darken the earth on a clear day,
& I will turn your feasts into mourning,
& all your songs into lamentation,

& I will bring mourning clothes to all,
& shaving to every head,
& I will make it like the mourning for an only son,
& the end of everything will be a bitter day.

Look, the days are coming, YHWH says,
that I will send a famine on the land;

not a famine of bread,
nor a thirst for water,
but of hearing the words of YHWH.

Then you will wither from sea to sea,
from north to east; you will run to & fro
seeking the word of YHWH,

but you will not find the word.

On that day the young women

The Climactic Confrontation (Part II)

& young men will faint for thirst.

Those who swear by the wrongdoings of Samaria,
& say, your YHWH, O, Dan of the North, lives; &
the cult of Beer-sheba in the South lives;
even they will fall,

never to rise up again.

Living in the Realm of G-D

a Primer & Manifesto

You might say I moved out of the desert & into that Realm of G-D that Brother Jesus talks about. Happens. Brother John da Baptist did it the other way 'round. Happens.

It's a tough neighborhood, the Realm, the Beloved Community, Nirvana, whatever ya wanna call it. Only the crazies; only the artists & poets & prophets & saints live there when they're carbon-based. Only the ones who have stepped waaaay out, way out over the line. It's a mental kinda place, ya know.

> My allegiance is to my fellow citizens
> in the Realm of G-D—
> human, animal, plant, mineral.
> Justice. Compassion.
> All that is, seen & unseen.
>
> There, it's always Backwards Monday—
> the first is last, the last first; the high low;
>
> the list goes on, & the logic is simple:
> practice compassion.
> Every minute.
>
> There, there's a zero–tolerance policy on zero tolerance.
> There, lack of compassion gets no compassion.

Living in the Realm of G-D

Yes, I moved out of a little, backward place,
called Every Nation in Human History, &
into an expansive kingdom, beyond time,

living on a planet teeming with miracles—
animals, plants, minerals; miraculous atoms,

miraculous carbon
carbonating.

The passport is free. It's freedom.
Beyond self. Beyond. Beyond.
Thoroughly beyond.

Myth is Just Something That Happens Again & Again

Inside any myth, it gets real.
Just as a jail cell that holds its victim is real.
Just as a lie that traps its victim is true.

Inside the myth there are valleys,
if the myth needs valleys.
Inside the myth there are serpents,
if the myth needs serpents.

Only in myth is there any real real,
even though the real is constructed,
a story, a fiction,
as real always
must be.

The question is always
the question we need
answered now, in its faces
& facets. Always it's
wise to sit down & ask,
what is the problem that's
being perceived here?

Those who say what human beings
ought to do are lost already.
We do well, rather, to look at
what it is that human beings do do.

Myth is Just Something That Happens Again & Again

Can do and still be.

This is not pragmatism.
This is merely peering through
the valleys in the myth. Looking
out from the walls
of one myth onto
the serpents of another.

The "ought" myths are myriad.
The "do" myths are few.
The Greeks got it right
with their careening, amoral G-Ds:
these myths described
a place to sit, high
above human folly.

We people of the desert?
Our warrior G-Ds described
the violence so easy to unleash
in a glaring sun. Our G-Ds
describe so much about
"my people" this &
"my people" that.

The walls of myths.

& the current desert G-D,
one transcending borders yet
favoring this one or that? Ah,
myths! Inside the myth, is real.

Outside, only foolishness.
But peering through walls!
Myth upon myth . . .
O, prophets! O, poets!
Put on your X–ray specs!

Only the imagined is real.

The Skinny on the Real

By "real" I mean
"permanent."
Bro Heraclitus says

what is real is change.
& change again.

Lust. Hatred. Ignorance.
These dim the light
of pure mind,

until our minds fill
with concept
after concept;

until we see things
as having separate

essences. There's
the problem.
Essence. Reality.

There is no other
after essence.
No second. No plural.

Nothing.

The Climactic Confrontation (Part III)

Sure, I saw them picking up the stones. I knew that it's unwise to walk to the temple, the cathedral, the church, the bastions of the prejudices & power & speak truth. What's new? Only my mind, my dears.

Sure, I knew you never turn your back on a priest.

Sure, I saw them picking up stones. I knew the crowd; the populace will follow the money & the power. I knew that the priest only had to say the word. But I said the truth anyway:

> I saw YHWH standing beside the altar.
> YHWH said, Smite the lintel of the door
> So that the posts shatter & smash
> onto the heads of the people.
>
> I will slay the last of them with the sword.
> Those who run will not get away.
>
> No one shall escape.
> Though they dig into hell itself,
> even there I will find them;
>
> though they climb up to heaven,
> from there I will bring them down.
>
> Though they hide on top of Mount Carmel,
> I will search them out & take them from there.
>
> Though they hide from my sight
> at the bottom of the sea,

The Art of Prophecy

there I will come with the serpent,
& he will bite them.

Though they be driven
into captivity by their enemies,
thence will I come with the sword,
& it will slay them.

I will set my eyes upon them to do evil, not good.

So the Blood

So the priestly-priest Amaziah
took the first shot, just to
say it was all OK.

& the stones rained down.
& my blood returned to the rocks.
& my carbon hit the road,

out to the cosmos or wherever
this is for another round.

I'd like to say it's not so bad, being stoned.
I'd like to say it's not so bad, dying for truth.

But I won't lie to you.

Of BS & Utopias

The deep question is where justice comes from.

Let's just say there's a cold rain fallin'.
Now. Are you in it or no?
Are you in it & you don't wanna be?
How long?

Let's just say.

Now. Who's to say you should or shouldn't be in that long cold rain?

The copout answer is "G-D wills it." Cop out. If you think that, do not pass go. Go get a life.

I've never seen the world from the vantage point of "this is as it is just because it is."

Call me utopian! (Yes, using utopia or the past always functions as wish fulfillment, but so does saying things are as they are because they have to be!)

Don't think I haven't had some talks with that Gang of Four everybody calls Brother Laozi.

Truth to tell, I like the Laozi Gang & The Way a lot better than what passes for Judeo or Christian! What ticks me about the Bros Laozi is that in their book, everything is all about the past & all about the top of the pyramid.

Of BS & Utopias

All this stuff about the old days & "the leader" this & the "wise leader" that. I call BS, bros.

See, the way of every cheat, from Laozi to me to wherever you're living, is to point to another time, an ideal time that never wuz. It might be a Golden Age. That's Laozi. It might be the Day of YHWH, that's me. It might be Progress; that's probably you. Or "The Future."

If our hopes & dreams are for large groups of human beings—call it nation or society—then we're going to be belly–achin' about now because of a past or a future that's pretty cool. Pretty happening.

Brother Buddha & his boys (& girls) jump off that band wagon & say it's all about now & all about the I that doesn't exist.

Cop out.

Anybody who's bit into a peach gone bad knows you can live all up into the now, as long as the next bite is tasty. When it's not, the now turns nasty.

Same thing with that Golden Age somewhere in the past. Question is always *when*. Last week? Ten years ago? Who was it had the grimace so that the other person could smile?

You wanna put that eu–topia so far in the future that it's in another world? Sooner or later someone's gonna take a sniff of that pie in the sky & say it's rancid.

What then?

Gonna deny what everybody can smell?

Am I so totally idealistic that I think that it's intelligent—nay—common sense—that carbon-based creatures who sign onto a project ought to have some hope of seeing its completion? Why should I put my hand to the plow without having at least a reasonable assurance that I know who will reap the harvest?

If not me, then at least someone I might reasonably wish to reap the fruit of my labor?

So, seems to me, it's reasonable to ask where the Golden Age or Eternity is, exactly. & if you're saying "can't touch it," it's reasonable for me to say, "BS, buddy. Pull the other one."

Deliver. That's the catchword I suggest to anyone listening to a line about a better world. Deliver. Or show me how the hell that could possibly work out.

The Danger is in Not Being You

There is a story about Rabbi Zushya who, when he was dying, told his students that he was very afraid.

The students were shocked & said, "But rabbi, you have always told us that YHWH is full of love & kindness!"

"I'm not afraid of YHWH," said Rabbi Zushya. "I know that YHWH will not ask me why I was not Moses or Isaiah. I'm afraid that YHWH will ask me why I wasn't Zushya."

From what I'm seein' of timelessness, you ain't gonna be asked why you didn't do it like Moses or Jesus or Mohammed or Gandhi.

But all you got when you're not carbon-based is you. So, as Bro Francis de Sales puts it, "Be who you are & be that perfectly well."

Look and see it: You didn't choose who you are in the carbon-based realm. I sure as hell didn't wanna be a shepherd from Tekoa who went off and got his ass kicked and his back stabbed and his brain smashed in the street.

Just sayin'.

You wanna find YHWH or whatever other g-d you're lookin' for? Don't be projectin' yer projections on the sky.

All the g-ds are only human ways of turnin' Brother Hume's "is" to an "ought."

The Art of Prophecy

Just a couple a rules of thumb: One, you ain't "g-d." Two, you're a tiny little bit in a great big awesome whole; and three, everything's gonna be all right—it don't hurt all that long.

The Practice of Spiritual Justice

> Oh, human, YHWH has shown you what is good;
> What does YHWH require of you
>
> but to do justice, love kindness,
> & walk humbly with your G–D?
> (Micah 6:8)

I'm gonna preach it:

One way to know a position is misguided is that it needs to be defended.

The absolute and in-born worth of every person does not need to be defended. It is a truth.

That the "all that is" is woven in "an inextricable web of mutuality" does not need to be defended. It is a truth.

Human purpose and meaning is to realize & act on truths.

To live in integrity with all that is, we must act for the good of all that is, even if the powers-that- be are pickin' up them stones to chuck at you.

Much of all that is is viewed in worldly—non-spiritual—comprehension as Other—whether that be mineral, animal, human. Spiritual integrity says that there is no Other. As Brother Mohammed said, "Wheresoever you turn, there is the face of Allah." (*Qur'an* 2:109).

The Art of Prophecy

That's that kid's yer lookin' at over there. That old guy's face. That sexy person's face. That adder's face. That sheep's face.

And, that's your face you're lookin' at too.

Wherever you come from, find yer freedom, get yer liberation of yourself, then, if you really and truly freed yourself, you're gonna love everything—and I mean everything—enough to want to free that everything else too. 'Cause there ain't nothin' else. It's all one big "we."

The meaning and the purpose of being carbon-based is compassion & justice.

The means are compassion & justice.

The end is integrity, compassion, non–violence, & oneness with all that is.

The means are integrity, compassion, non–violence & oneness with all that is.

Action produces conflict; the challenge is to direct conflict toward the goal of liberation.

The past is past; the past is prologue; the now is the only place there can be any action.

Relationship, relationship, relationship. Right relation. Relationship.

There is good spiritual discipline in seeing the water we swim in. Yet fish can't change their water. They are likely to accept it as "the nature of things" or even if they say the water is nasty—they're gonna swim in it.

First we must see. Then we must act. Both seeing & acting are continuous spiritual practice. Yea, you know I'm gonna say "praxis."

The spiritual praxis is not about working for a vague and high-minded tomorrow. The praxis is embodying compassion & justice each and every moment—right there in your carbon form. Living in the Beloved Community means embodying it. Liberation of all that is.

The Practice of Spiritual Justice

You wanna be a prophet? There's the door!

Next Steps, Brother Rilke Style

You must
change
your life.

You Have You

Nothin' that matters is
beyond time & space;

all that matters is
within time & space;

if you can't feel
in yer time & space,

you have *you*
to lose.

The Big Blank Sky

What if being unknown is YHWH's point?
What if not existing is YHWH's point?

What if being the projection screen for our passions, wishes, & fears is YHWH's point?
What if that's the point of all the g–ds?

I've had so many years. & I've never yet seen the Big Guy (or Big Gal or Big It or Big They).
After so long, revolving under the sun, I don't even know where the head office is if I decided to go there.

Gives ya pause, ya know? Made me a Kabbalist at least, you know? But who has time to read all that, with so many fruits to help ripen?

"Is there a G=D?" has never been the meaningful question, IMHO.

Look around, and you'll see G-Ds everywhere: Pride. Ego. Mercedes. Fiat.

> Moolah.
> Sex.
>
> G-Ds,
> G-Ds,
> G-Ds.
>
> There's sooo many G-Ds,
> some of them called YHWH.

The Big Blank Sky

Some of 'em called . . .
Makes ya wanna be
a . . . non–theist, ya know?

Radical, that.
Plumb holy. That.
Trim the options
down to zero.

Gives ya pause, ya know? &, sister, don't we fill the space of that blank screen, blank canvas, blank page, blank wall, blank sky . . . with a few too many thoughts? Thoughts when we coulda been doin' something.

Take a Persian rug. A rug from India is still a rug, no?

Or a chair. An Italian chair & a Russian chair & a Brazilian chair. All chairs. All tools.

Are there any eternal myths? Persian G–D. Indian G–D. Italian G–D. Is there an eternal G–D? No. No more than there are eternal persons. Or eternal empires. Or eternal cities.

Only nothing is eternal.

Some myths go a good way toward doing nearly–permanent good, though. Here's one that works:

The Sufi one, *La illa ha il Allah hu*—there is only Allah. Say that three times!

> La illa ha il Allah hu.
> La illa ha il Allah hu.
> La illa ha il Allah hu.

Another that works: there is no G–D at all.

Yes, after a while you see that all religions are as right as rain as far as any partial vision goes. Yet you know, there's no "rightness" in rain. It merely falls. It's merely essential, in moderate amounts in the right spot.

The Art of Prophecy

But we desert folks, we do alright too.

So many lives. So much pride. So many names. So much oppression.

Makes ya wanna be a prophet!

If you do, go, with my blessings!

I hope I've helped a little bit.

OK, I'll Say It

The Problem of Existence

The problem of existence
calls like a redwing
blackbird from a
bent stalk
at the field's edge.

The problem of existence
treads water;

the problem of existence
sinks;

the problem of existence
sings like a redwing
blackbird from

a bent stalk at
the field's edge.

I'll Buy Ya a Drink in Nearly–Eternity

I'm in a pub & a young woman a bit tipsy is going on & on about San Francisco. So I know I'm not in San Francisco.

I *like* Brother Francis, actually. Lots of the locals don't. Sister Hildegarde can't stand him. It's true that he does have that Brother Jerry Garcia vibe, speaking of San Francisco.

It's not that I don't like hippies.

Have I explained enough about the Afterlife? It's not like there's a heaven & hell & all that. At least not wherever I am.

It's all this big ball, rolled into one. Like everything else. Brother Attila is here. He has his kaffeeklatsch. They're fine folks.

It's not that I want to hang out with other major minor poets. Brother Micah? He's all about destruction. Habakuk still whinin'? Gimme a break! It's not like he's not a fine fella. But think about how it is in nearly-eternity. Do I want to hang with other BCE people or do I talk with other people from other times?

Sure, there's some nostalgia going on with others who consider sheep's eyes a delicacy. Still, what would *you* do if you had the choice between hearing Habakuk talking about locusts for the 9997th time, or you can buy Brother Kurt Cobain another beer & hear some rockin' acoustic folk.

There are worse places than nearly-eternity. Trust me. But getting here *is* a bitch. No doubt. And no choice in the matter.

Being Nearly Timeless
(& Being & Time, Take 5)

    Live as if it matters;
    because it does.
    The train has left the station;
    the plane is off the ground;
    the Eagle has landed;
    that ship has sailed.
    It's all been chewed down
    to the last stick of gum.
    Your cleverness won't
    get you nothing.
    It's already dead!

Some nights for the open mic, Brother David plays his harp at the pub & Brother Jesus sits in with his hammer 'n' saw. They will get down on one of my favorites,

    Wait just a little while longer
    & the wicked will be no more;
    you'll look everywhere for 'em

    but they won't be anywhere!
    Yes, the meek will inherit the land
    & dance in the abundance! (37:10–11)

You've been sleep walking.

Don't go back to sleep.

The Art of Prophecy

Don't go back to sleep.

P.S. When you journey out beyond mind & time, look me up. I'll buy the first round.
(Just kiddin' about "buying." Ain't no money 'round here.)

Postlude

OK, ya got me—I've still got that ego thing goin' on.
Brother Zhuangzi disappeared from here. It can happen. It's rare. The imprint of our carbon-based lives is so damn deep. We *can* get past ourselves, though. It happens. Brother Zhuangzi told this story:

> Imagine you are crossing a river in a boat. Suddenly, an empty boat hits yours. Even if you are in a bad mood, you will not become very angry at the motiveless actions of an empty boat.
>
> Now imagine that a person is in the boat that hit you. You will shout, "Hey, stupid, watch out!"
>
> If the person doesn't respond, you will shout louder. All because there is someone in the boat.
>
> Empty boat, no anger.
> Person in the boat, anger.
>
> Now, what if you can imagine all the other boats empty. And then, yours too. Your boat empty as you cross the river of the world. Then, no one will oppose you; no one will seek to harm you.
>
> Empty your boat.

Yes, that's what I'm workin' on. Emptying my boat of the anger at poverty, fame, power. Emptying my boat of all my self and my petty angers and resentments. So that I, like my brother Zhuangzi, may someday disappear into the One, if there is such a thing. The One. Which is nothing. And everything. And nothing. And.
"Poof."

(Repeating) Amos's Famous Qualifications for Being a Prophet:

1. Be an empty vessel.
2. Have no talents and few brains.
3. Be a misfit no one has ever understood.
4. Tell your truth even if it appears to be (even to yourself) nonsense.
5. Tell your truth loud and straight—as you see it, even if it looks daft, mad, or insane.
6. Prepare to die.

About the Author

Rev. Dr. David Breeden has a Master of Fine Arts in poetry from The Iowa Writers' Workshop and a PhD from the Center for Writers at the University of Southern Mississippi, with additional study in writing and Buddhism at Naropa Institute in Boulder, Colorado. He also has a Master of Divinity degree from Meadville Lombard Theological School. He is a certified Humanist Celebrant.

Breeden has published many books of poetry and translations.

After a career as an English professor, Breeden was ordained into the Unitarian Universalist ministry in 2008. He serves on the Education Committee of the American Humanist Association. He serves as adjunct faculty at Meadville Lombard Theological School. He is an Associate member of The Institute for American Religious and Philosophical Thought. He is Senior Minister at First Unitarian Society of Minneapolis, a historically humanist congregation.

David blogs at https://medium.com/@davidbreeden7
He tweets at @dbreeden.

www.ingramcontent.com/pod-product-compliance
Lightning Source LLC
Chambersburg PA
CBHW050350230426
43663CB00010B/2068